Research on the Laws of Contemporary China

Volume 1: 1949-1978

Editor-in-chief Chen Su

Translated By He Jingjing[1] and Shang Cong[2]

Paths International Ltd

中国社会科学出版社
CHINA SOCIAL SCIENCES PRESS

1 Dr. He Jingjing is an Assistant Researcher at the Institute of International Law, the Chinese Academy of Social Sciences

2. Dr. Shang Cong is a licensed lawyer in both State of California and People's Republic of China

Biography of Editor-In-Chief

CHEN Su, a research fellow in the Institute of Law of Chinese Academy of Social Sciences, and a doctoral supervisor, graduated from Liaoning University in 1985 as a bachelor of law; from the Institute of Law of Chinese Academy of Social Sciences in 1988 as a degree of master of law. At present he has held the office of the Co-Secretary of the Party Committee of the Institute of, and the Research Center of the Chinese Academy of Social Sciences; and executive director of China Law Society and Vice Chairman of the Commercial Jurisprudence Research Society.

He has mainly specialized in civil and commercial law, with works and writings, such as *Special Research on Securities Law*, *Exploration on Subtle Logic of Spirit of Law*, *New Development of Society Law*; and with dozens of papers published in professional academic journals such as *Chinese Journal of Law* and *China Legal Sciences*.

Preface

Just like the history of the PRC, the study of jurisprudence over the past 60 years since 1949 has been prosperous through hard times, developing steadily and making brilliant achievements with each passing day. The book describes China's jurisprudence study over the past 60 years in general terms, showing the status and evolution process of the new China's jurisprudence in various development stages, analyzing the background and reason for the formation and evolution of important theories in the course of studying jurisprudence, and manifesting theoretical achievements in development and prosperity of jurisprudence and their practical value. It is expected that the book help readers have a clear impression on the development path of China's jurisprudence, to learn the experience of researchers who have devoted their hard efforts and wisdoms to the development process of China's jurisprudence, and to experience the impulse of the "rule of law" era along with the development of the PRC.

General Introduction

The world today is the midst of unprecedented drastic changes, whereas China has the strategic opportunity of promoting the socialism modernization development with chinese characteristics — a critical period for building well-off society in an all-around way, and for the reform and opening-up. All of above have provided the studies of philosophy and social sciences with great opportunities to attain great prosperity and development. Currently, the development of philosophy and social science enjoy three big advantages: firstly the laudable practice of the Chinese-characteristic socialist development, which provides broad arena, i.e., plenty of opportunities, to the field of philosophy and social science; a steady flow of resources and materials to the research of philosophy and social science; second, the Communist Party of China and the state's strong commitment and support, which guarantees the prosperity and development of philosophy and social science; third, the implementation of the policy of "Encouraging blossoming and contending of all", which creates a favorable environment for new thinking and theory innovation in the field of philosophy and social sciences.

It was clearly put forward in China's "Twelfth Five-year Development Plan Outline" that "promote the building of the philosophy and social sciences innovation system, and implement the philosophy and social sciences innovation project, with prosperity and development of the philosophy and social sciences". And in response to the call the Academy of Social Sciences launched the philosophy and social sciences innovation project, a project designed to make efforts to achieve the innovation based on the direction of Marxism of the philosophy and social sciences system—the innovation mainly involving academic viewpoints and theories, academic disciplines, scientific research organization and management, scientific research methods and means, and personnel systems. The purpose to implement innovation project is to establish the philosophy and social science innovation system, to continue to strengthen research of the philosophy and social science, to produce more high quality results that can stand up to practice test, and to develop high-level talents with proper political ideology, and clear academic direction, all to serve the people, prosperous development of advanced socialist civilization, and the socialism with Chinese characteristics.

One of the important contents to implement innovation project is to follow the natural principles of philosophy and social science research to perfect discipline establishment mechanism, optimize discipline structure, and shape a discipline layout meeting China's needs with Chinese characteristics, reasonable structure and prominent advantages. As a means of displaying great achievements of innovation project, the writing of development reports on varied disciplines of the philosophy and social science, as for accurate grasp of academic frontier development, and for active advance of discipline establishment and innovation, is an important job with long-term fundamental importance.

Since the establishment of the People's Republic of China, the philosophy and social science system with Chinese characteristics has been in the course of its formation and development, in the history of Chinese socialistic revolution, construction and reform and development. Especially since the reform and opening-up, with China's economic and social development, the research on varied disciplines of the philosophy and social science has been expanded and deepened continuously, making remarkable achievements and attracting worldwide attention. In order to promote the further development in idea, method and system of philosophy and social science with Chinese characteristics, style and manner, and to drive excellent achievements and talents of China's philosophy and social science to go to the world, who should more actively participate in international academic dialogues, and raise the voice of China's philosophy and social sciences, so as to strengthen the soft power of Chinese culture, it is urgent to sort out academic ideas in varied disciplines of the philosophy and social science, and to summarize excellent accumulated results of the disciplines, including the proposition of major academic point of views and its impacts, the formation and evolution of important academic schools, the writing and publishing of important academic books and literature, and the emergence of the large numbers of important representative academic figures. Hence, the China Social Sciences Press has organized and compiled a large-scale series of consecutively-published books, the Report on Disciplinary Development of China's Philosophy and Social Sciences, which is not merely a great event in academic circle, but an important part of the philosophy social science innovation project, too.

The Report on Disciplinary Development of China's Philosophy and Social Sciences is divided into two subseries: *Annual Reviews* and *Frontier Reports*, the former published annually as first-level discipline; the latter published every three years, both consecutively-published in compiled-book form. Contents of the *Annual Reviews* include the latest trends at home and aboard in the current year of the discipline development, important theory viewpoints and methods, hot issues and representative scholars and their masterpieces; contents of the *Frontier Reports* overall status of the discipline development, concerns and matters at home and aboard over the past three years of academic frontier dynamics, the latest theory viewpoints and methods, significant theory innovation and hot issues, and main representative personage and their masterpieces on academic frontier at home and aboard. Each discipline development report should be a high-level and –quality research result, reflecting development and evolution contexts of contemporary important thoughts of disciplines and academies; fruits from hard work in tracking research of the discipline by the author for a long time; and mirror recent development trends of the discipline, to hold accurately academic foreland and to guide disciplinary development. Therefore we believe that the implementation of this publication project will certainly play an important role in promoting construction and development of the various disciplines of the philosophy and social sciences in China, and that the series of books will become important historical literature and teaching materials in academic research of the philosophy and social science, making a significant contribution to China's research of philosophy and social sciences, education and talent preparation.

Table of Contents

Volume I 1949-1978

Volume II 1978-1992

Volume I 1949-1978

Research on the Laws of Contemporary China

Volume I 1949-1978

Introduction

In this Part, we choose 1949 as the starting point and 1978 the end point of this period. It is obvious that 1949 was the founding year of the People's Republic of China, from which every matter of importance in political life (including jurisprudence) in Chinese society all turned over a new leaf and accordingly China's jurisprudence turned out to be entirely different from what it had been; 1978 was the starting point of China's Reform and Opening, from which the road of socialism with Chinese characteristics got started and accordingly, again, everything regarding China's jurisprudence turned out to be entirely different from the past. But the above two turns definitely do not mean that China's jurisprudence went back to the original point after nearly thirty years, instead, they show that China's jurisprudence has selected a way toward a brand-new, identifiable and contemporary road to happiness, which is different from what it had been prior to 1949 as well as prior to 1978.

Although the years can be clearly classified, the existing form and evolution process of the theory of China's jurisprudence could not be classified so clearly by years, for example, scholars studying criminal jurisprudence are inclined to treat the promulgation of 1979 Criminal Law as the start of revival of criminal jurisprudence; while scholars in constitutional jurisprudence are more willing to consider the promulgation of 1982 Constitution as the beginning of the new era of constitutional jurisprudence. However, taking the whole history of new China into consideration, those two years can be placed as a symbol for classification of the development stages of the jurisprudence in that period. The reason is that the political events which occurred in those two years not only completely changed the overall perception and social trends of China, but also altered the formation of fundamental concepts and systems of China's jurisprudence. Of course, such periodization merely has academic significance, because description of the development process of China's jurisprudence may exceed such period limit due to the continuity and relevance of historical events. For example, the formation of systematic perception when drawing up the *Common Program of the Chinese People's Political Consultative Conference* was actually derived from the period prior to 1949; while the theoretical impact on the formation of China's jurisprudence imposed by the U. S. S. R. lasts after 1978.

When referring to the period between 1949 and 1978, a sigh may be the only possible outcome from the perspective of legal history because the history failed to grant a minimum favor to China's jurisprudence. Disorder in political life in Chinese society and the fact that the country was completely occupied by the ideology of the paramountcy of the class struggle made China's jurisprudence neither rely on systematic legal system nor be included by ideogenetic knowledge system. However, it is not exactly the truth. Although the country governance and social operation were dominated by the ideology of the paramountcy of the class struggle and highly centralized planned economic system, the legal system still played roles to some extent, more or less, stronger or weaker. Accordingly, there was still space for the survival and development of jurisprudence. Definitely, the survival space for jurisprudence was rather cramped and the opportunity for the development of jurisprudence very transient. Firstly, laws still existed. For example, the Constitution was still effective (despite its existence was only legal formally during the Cultural Revolution) and the Marriage Law could still work. Secondly, jurisprudence still existed. Although jurisprudence was attached in the theory system of nation and law, some people still diligently annotated the existing laws or introduced legal theories of the U. S. S. R. Thirdly, legal education still existed. Some colleges had legal courses, in spite of their poor content and discrete education progress. The seed of Chinese jurisprudence was passed on from then on, which made the jurisprudential circle encounter a booming development after China's reform and opening. To sum up, jurisprudence during this period presented a down curve: laws were kept more and more uncultivated, jurisprudence more and more desolated and the legal talents more and more withered. Fortunately, China's jurisprudence survives. It is necessary to look back and rethink profoundly due to the past.

In this period, the alternate popularity of legal instrumentalism and legal nihilism directly resulted in the rough survival of legal theory. Whether in concept of nation governing or choice of policies, no continuous views on law came into being; on the contrary, the concept of 'rule by man' was upheld. What the leaders said is considered as 'law' while being against the words of the leaders as 'violation of law'. Laws changed as the words of the leaders altered.[1] In the early 1950s, as the construction of national system began to receive more attentions, the Constitution and the Marriage Law were promulgated and implemented accordingly; in late 1950s, based on the convenience of 'rule by man' and the changes of social situation, laws became futile. In early 1960s, based on the introspection of previous policy mistakes and changes of social situation, laws were paid attention again and obtained a slim chance of survival and some legislative work was put on the agenda; however, from the mid-1960s, due to the change of judgment on social situation and reselection of nation governing policies, laws were abandoned again at once. Accordingly, legal instrumentalism and legal nihilism are the twinborn concepts grown from the same root. Law is useful when taken as an appropriate instrument of politics and futile when taken as an inappropriate instrument of politics. In a social environment where legal instrumentalism and legal nihilism are alternatively popular, a real jurisprudence could not be formed, because the legal instrumentalism makes the jurisprudence

1 *Selected Works of DENG Xiaoping*, p.146, People's Publishing House, 1994.

vulgar while legal nihilism makes it groundless.

During this period, China's jurisprudence has not become an independent theoretic system or subject system. The status of the jurisprudence of that time is characterized by 'dual lacks of independence'. On one hand, in the aspect of knowledge system, jurisprudence of that time was only an appendage of the politics, as a branch theory of relevant doctrines under the cover of the theory of nation and law. Jurisprudence was only an explanation about law as a phenomenon of the political science. Jurisprudence prior to China's Reform and Opening was called "jurisprudence of politics and laws", which was actually dominated and led by political theories.1 Therefore, whether in subject constitution or theory system, China's jurisprudence did not exist independently. Secondly, in the aspect of sources of knowledge, the academic system of China's jurisprudence mainly came from the overall inheritance of the jurisprudence theory of the U. S. S. R., which caused the overdependence on the jurisprudence theory of the U. S. S. R. by China's jurisprudence. The Chinese theoretical circles at this time was in lack of capacity of interpreting socialistic views of law from Marxism, it could only accept the dogmatized and biased so-called 'Marxism Views of Laws' which had been explained by scholars from the U. S. S. R. in advance in the process of inheriting the jurisprudence theory of the U. S. S. R.. In addition, the capacity of constructing independently China's own legal knowledge system was also absent. Recalling the jurisprudence theory of that time, everything was inherited from the U. S. S. R., including the definition of legal concepts, construction of legal system, recognition of the legal mechanism, the way how jurisprudence instructs the legal practice, and the transfer of the material carrier used for delivering those legal theories. For example, during the first decade from the founding of the new China, 165 translation books were published, most of which were legal works and

1 *Report on Development of Philosophy and Social Science in China's Colleges and Universities·Jurisprudence (1978-2008)*, ZHANG Wenxian (chief editor) and HUANG Wenyi (subeditor), p.4, Guangxi Normal University Publishing House, 2008.

textbooks of the U. S. S. R..1The ideological impact on China's jurisprudence by jurisprudence of the U. S. S. R. is highly profound and lasting, which was not repelled as China and the U. S. S. R. became enemies later, but instead eliminating the superficial 'U. S. S. R.' label, the theoretical substance still the same. Objectively speaking, though, the inheritance of the jurisprudence of the U. S. S. R. by China's jurisprudence community was selective to some extent. For example, introduction of the theory of economic laws from the U. S. S. R. was rare. The reason for the rarity is worthy analysis, which is that the planned economy of China, in its nature, repelled the introduction of legal system, so there was no room for talking about the economic law theory then.

The core theoretical mainstream of China's jurisprudence in that period is the political concept and national theory of the paramountcy of the class struggle. Like considering the law as a political instrument for class struggle, jurisprudence was also considered as the extension of the theory of class struggle or professionally refined theory of class struggle. When the nature of class becoming the essential attributes of laws, the theory of class struggle accordingly became the core theory of jurisprudence and the logical cornerstone of legal studies development. Therefore, 'the argument, deduction, conclusion, structure and system of jurisprudence, and the collecting, analysis, use of the legal materials and literatures, as well as the manner and wording of writing were all revolving the axis of 'nature of class', and the jurisprudence became 'the studies of class struggle'. ... Putting "nature of class" as the cornerstone, frame of reference or conceptual mode of jurisprudence will definitely make the jurisprudence losing the competence as well as standing as an independent subject.'[2]As the mindset of the jurisprudence of that time, legal phenomenon was considered as the reflection of class struggle and interpreted according the theory of class struggle,

1 *Forty Years of China's Jurisprudence*, ZHANG Youyu (chief editor) and WANG Shuwen (subeditor), p.5, Shanghai People's Publishing House, 1989.

2 "Consciousness, System of Category and Cornerstone Category," ZHANG Wenxian, *Legal Studies*, Issue 3, 1991.

the function of laws was taken as the instrument of class struggle and accepted or rejected according to the method of class struggle, and the legal studies was certainly the theoretical activities serving the class struggle. When the law was no longer needed as the instrument of class struggle in the 'Cultural Revolution', jurisprudence was also snubbed and thrown to the isolated corner in society.

One outstanding feature of the theoretical forming and knowledge system constructing of China's jurisprudence of that time was focusing on getting rid of the old while ignoring setting up the new. From the founding of the new China, to eliminate the 'views of old laws' became an important political task and theoretical precondition of the construction of legal system and studies. To construct a brand-new regime must be accompanied by eliminating the outdated regime including laws and the attached ideology, so to critique the 'views of old laws' was an inevitable political choice and fundamental policy direction. But the outcome of criticizing and eliminating the 'views of old laws' could not definitely lead to a new construction of China's jurisprudence. Setting aside inheriting the jurisprudence theory of the U. S. S. R., China's own jurisprudence system was not established in that period. Certainly, it is not historically practical to require people at that time to achieve this from today's perspective. However, other than the lack of practical experience and theoretical preparation of socialist rule of law at that time, the political decision of inappropriate treatment on laws and jurisprudence also heavily hindered the independent formation and continuous development of China's jurisprudence. In late 1950s, the jurisprudence area became a harder-hit area of anti-rightist struggle. Some people who had correct viewpoints or came up with valuable suggestions to construction of democracy and rule of law were classified as rightists as considered to have spoken wrong or offensive expressions; some legal theoretical issues, such as fundamental principles or specific systems, became forbidden zones for discussion.[1] When people today have to search for legal academic concerns and theoretical intelligence from what

1 *Forty Years of China's Jurisprudence*, ZHANG Youyu (chief editor) and WANG Shuwen (subeditor), p.6, Shanghai People's Publishing House, 1989.

the rightists said in publications of that time, we may feel somewhat distressed as stroking the wound of history.

However, it is also partial and biased if we just come to negative judgment and critical conclusion from the formation and change of China's jurisprudence of that time. Admittedly, China at that time lacked practical experience and theoretical preparation of socialist rule of law, while the legal practice of the U. S. S. R. is the closest experience of socialist laws and its legal theory is the newest interpretation of Marxism views of laws, so to inherit legal theories of the U. S. S. R. was the most reasonable and convenient choice for China then. However, the problem is that China's jurisprudence lost itself when inheriting the legal theories of the U. S. S. R. It is also acknowledged that the class struggle was a necessary policy choice taking into account the social reality of China at that time; detour and setbacks were unavoidable when constructing socialist legal systems without having any experience. But the question is: why was the class struggle deemed as paramountcy and why did it last for such a long time? Why were the detour and setbacks so huge and lasting? Those taking the lead to sum up the experiences and lessons and rethink the merits and defects of China's jurisprudence of that time are legal workers and researchers who experienced the changeable social and political situations in that period. Hence we can see that in spite of setbacks and difficulties, the sequence of thought of China's jurisprudence is still continuous and the thinking of pursuing socialist rule of law never stops. As a matter of fact, the fundamental theory and dominant idea of contemporary China's jurisprudence, many concepts and methods which still exist in legal knowledge system now, the leading legal talents who play important roles later, the rapid recovery of construction of jurisprudence team after China's Reform and Opening, timely inheritance and continuation of legal knowledge and the prompt scale expansion of China's legal studies, etc., all rely on the accumulation and cultivation of that time. We, as successors, shall pay our respects to those legal researchers of that time who had the courage to explore in depth and insisted on independent thinking, and the contribution made by them on the theoretical accumulation and academic inheritance.

Chapter 1

Rough Start of China's Socialist Jurisprudence

1. Rise of Theory in China on "State and Law"

China is facing frequent and huge changes in 20th century. Reviewing China's history and even that of the world, perhaps there is no country like the China in 20th century, which has experienced so many—such as suffering and achievement, removal of old things and arrangement of new ones, and frustration and hope—in only one hundred years as have continually changed not only China's reality and history, but also behavior and ideology of Chinese people. The founding of New China is one of the greatest historical events in 20th century, which not just has set up brand new political system and law in Chinese history, but made legal views pertain to political system and law as well as jurisprudence directed thereunder get fire-new features and nature. Inception of legal views and jurisprudence system of socialism is formation and development of "Theory on State and Law" under the guidance of Marxism with distinct characteristics of socialist jurisprudence.

Owing to historical causes, deduction and derivation in China of socialist "Theory on State and Law" is not through publicity and direction in jurisprudence theory writings, or popularization by textbooks, but through implementation of policies and issuance of government decrees. In January 1949, the *Suggestion on Takeover of Kuomintang's Judiciary Authorities in Peking and Tianjin* announced that, "All the laws by Kuomintang (KMT) are invalid and it is forbidden to invoke any law by Kuomintang in criminal and civil cases. All the trials by a court shall be carried out in accordance with decrees issued by the Military Control Commission and policies by the People's Government". In September 1949, the *Common Program of Chinese People's Political Consultative Conference* provided that, "Abolish all the laws, decrees and judicial systems issued by the reactionary government of Kuomintang; enact laws and decrees to protect the people and establish the people's judicial system". Still, the *Instruction on Abolishing 'Pandect of Six Laws' of the kuomintang and Determining Judicial Doctrines for Liberated Area* issued in February 1949 is enough to explain legal theories to guide the foresaid decisions. It is necessary to quote key paragraphs from the Instruction as follows:

Law is a so-called national ideology to be enforced by the ruling class with armed forces, as is state, only an instrument to protect certain ruling class interests… Actually, since there is no state above classes, there is no law above classes… There is no true common interests between ruling class and ruled class, a man of property and proletarian, creditor and debtor; hence there are no really equal legal rights. Therefore, all the laws by the kuomintang could be only an instrument to protect reactionary ruling of landlords, comprador bureaucrats and bourgeoisie, and weapon to suppress and shackle the broad masses of the people. …Any reactionary law…must more or less contain certain so-called provisions to protect all the people, yet it just as a state itself is an irreconcilable product and expression of class struggle… Therefore, the *Pandect of Six Laws* should not be deemed as a law that is partly rather than essentially protective of the broad masses of people's interests because it contains certain so-called specious provisions to protect the broad masses of people's interests. …Under the people's democratic dictatorship led by the working class and based on the alliance of workers and peasants, the *Pandect of Six Laws* of the kuomintang should be abolished, and should no longer govern the legal process of the people, which shall be handled in accordance with the new laws of the people. And until such laws are enacted systematically, the judicial process of the people should be based on the Chinese Communist Party's policies as well as all kinds of programs, laws, orders, regulations and resolutions that have been enacted by the people's Government and the People's Liberation Army. Meanwhile, law enforcement authorities should educate and reform their cadres, in the spirit of despising and criticizing the *Pandect of Six Laws* of the kuomintang and other reactionary laws and decrees, together with laws and decrees of capitalism countries such as Europe, the United States Japan that are anti-people; and in a way of learning and mastering national and legal view of Marxism-Leninism and Mao Zedong thought, as well as policies of the new democracy, its programs, laws, orders, regulations and resolutions. Only in that way can we make our judicial work a part of organic ingredients of the work of the people's democratic regime.

This "instruction" has not merely been documents of government decrees concerning the abolishment of the *Pandect of Six Laws* of the kuomintang and ascertaining judicial principles in liberated areas, but also political statements declaring Marxist state governance philosophy and legal views. And it adequately reflects basic views on the theory of state and law; has a great influence on formulation and popularization of China's mainstream view of law in society, and construction and repletion of system of jurisprudence knowledge.

Roughly speaking, the theory of state and law contains mainly four basic theories, such as the origin, essence, function and development of the state and law. Generally speaking, the state and law is a product of the historical stage in the development of human society, and irreconcilable product of class contradictions; law reflects the ruling class' will based on certain material living conditions, and class domination is the essence of the state and law, with class nature being its essential attribute. A tool for class domination, the state and law is used by the ruling class for ruling the ruled class to maintain the overall interest of the ruling class. With the emergence and development of the socialist society, the class antagonism and class struggle will be no longer in existence, hence dying off the state and law finally. The four theories, notably the first three, are embedded to varying degrees in the *Instruction on Abolishing 'Pandect of Six Laws' of the kuomintang and Determining Judicial Doctrines for Liberated Area.*

The theory of the state and law, influenced by Soviet political and legal theories, is a set of knowledge system regarding the state and law based on the long-term revolution and struggle practice. The theory has been systematically introduced into China since the founding of the New China[1], becoming one of the leading theories during the first 30 years since the founding. In the 1960s, due to the change of the Sino-soviet relations and internal requirements for the development of the discipline, the theoretical cycle of jurisprudence has once seen some tendency to break away from the influence of Soviet legal theory—an effort however that has not developed into mainstream—so that China has used the course of jurisprudence written by itself. Historical summary and reflection on the 30th anniversary of the founding of the New China and the 60th anniversary of the Party building, along with the reform of the economic system, has created political and economic conditions for renewal of the juristic theory, due to which the theory of the state and law has been replacing by "basic theory of law" since the 1980s. Even so, in terms of viewpoints of theoretical system and of some essential theories, it is still clear that jurisprudence textbooks many years later have been affected by the theory of the state and law.

1 Translated works for the time mainly include: the *Theory Tutorial of Marxism-Leninism about State and Legal Force*, co-authored by scientific researchers of the Soviet Academy of Sciences Institute of Law Science, published by China Renmin University Press, 1950; [Soviet]Denissow, the *Theory of the State and Law*, Zhonghua Book Company, 1951; [Soviet]Vyshinskii, the *Theoretical Issues on State and Law*, Law Press China, 1955, which effected most the jurisprudence theory of the initial period of New China; [Soviet]the *Theory of State and Law*, co-edited by Romashkin, Strogovik and Туманов, Law Press China, 1963. During 1960s to 80s, works titled "Theory of State and Law" in the Soviet Union had been published one by one, and some scholars in China paid close attention to such works.

As for theoretical origin, the theory of the state and law at bottom originates from Marx's discussion on the state, revolution, law, "right of capitalist class" and "transition period". Elucidated and deduced during the Soviet Union period, the theory system of the state and law mainly makes its logic start from the political formation during the political transition period of "proletarian dictatorship", of which the theoretical task is to research and resolve the questions of theory in political and legal practice in the wake of the proletariat taking the state power. With respect to historical stages or steps in the aftermath of the proletariat taking the state power, Marx hasn't elaborate demonstration and guidance, therefore, the theory of the state and law is divided in the basis of the subsequent historical practice and according to the existing form of the state into three stages: first, of "dictatorship of the proletariat"; second, of "a state of the entire people"; third, of "withering away of the state" and "social self-governance".[1] Historically, China's theory of the state and law has always rested on the stage of "dictatorship of the proletariat".

As to the "transition stage" of "dictatorship of the proletariat", Marx, learning from the failure lesson of Paris Commune, emphasizes the necessity of a state existing, which has been emphasized in the theory of the state and law for a rather long time. A basis point of the theory of the state and law, the "proletariat dictatorship state" is deemed as the early form of socialist state. To a large extent, the class antagonism and the suppression of the exploiting classes are the important reason for the existence of the "proletariat dictatorship state", judging from which, the class ruling and the class struggle are considered to be one of the essential functions of the state and law during this period. To the bourgeoisie's law, Marx and Engels pointed out in the *Communist Manifesto* that "Your own ideas are a product of the production and ownership relations of the bourgeois; just as your law is no more than those parts of the will of your class that have been

1 See the *Theory of State and Law*, co-edited by Romashkin, Strogovik and Tumanov, Law Press China, 1963, pp.214-246.

elevated into law, and the content of the will be determined by material living conditions of your class"[1]. Such a view on bourgeois law had been generalized in the "proletarian dictatorship" period, and the class ruling and the class struggle had also been identified as one of the primary functions of socialist law, as a result of which a typical definition about law is as follows: "Law—guaranteed to be put into force by the state, with compelling force, whose purpose is to protect, consolidate and develop social relations and orders favorable and comfortable to the ruling class—is the total sum of the rule of conduct giving expression to in the form of legislation the will of the ruling class, customs recognized by the state power, and public life rules."[2] Such a definition has had a huge impact on the theory of the state and law, the definition that is still adopted in some of China's jurisprudence textbooks and works many years later. However, this definition has received criticism in both the former Soviet Union and in China, mainly stemming from being qualitative and positioning of the socialist state and law in the new historical period.

In the theory of the state and law, notably the Soviet Union state and law theory, the "proletariat dictatorship" just is a ruling form at transition stage, that is, upon the completion of the socialist revolution and socialist transformation, the "proletariat dictatorship state" will become "a state of the entire people" where there is no longer class antagonism and class dominance, hence the socialist society into a period of "a state of the entire people". In this period, now that the structure of binary opposition and ruling will be no longer in existence in a state between the ruling class and ruled class, the class ruling function will no longer be considered applicable to the socialist state and its law. For this point, some Soviet scholars have pointed out, "It is not allowed to apply indiscriminately 'a state is a tool for class violence' to a socialist state (in particular for the stage when the socialist state becomes an organization of the entire people). So is exactly the socialist law. When the law is defined as the compulsory code of conduct to

1 *Marx and Engels' Anthology*, Vol. 1, People's Publishing House, 1955, p.289.
2 Vyshinskii, the *Theoretical Issues on State and Law*, Law Press China, 1955, p.100.

reflect the will of the ruling class and be guaranteed by the power of the state, this definition does not reflect the characteristics of socialist law. Therefore, it is correct for law of the exploiting classes, but incorrect for being applied indiscriminately to the socialist law, especially to the law for the period when socialism has won victory, during which the law has become a universal law"[1]. In spite of it, the socialist states have not died during this period. If the domestic class antagonisms provide the main reason for the existence of the "proletariat dictatorship state", then in the new historical period, the reason for "a state of the entire people" to exist in the form of "a state" mainly lies in the worldwide opposition between the socialist camp and the capitalist camp. This kind of state and law theory has a great influence on China's jurisprudence theory and legal practice.

In China, the theory of the state and law has roughly experienced periods as follows. First, it is from the time when the New China was founded in 1949 to the socialist transformation period in 1956 that the theory of the state and law was copied from the Soviet Union to China. During this period, jurisprudence theory was weak and backward, with a serious shortage of autonomy due to copying the Soviet Union, but with some development as compared to stagnate and dilapidation of political turmoil afterwards, for example, setting up of a batch of departments of politics and law as well as publications, cultivating of a group of students of politics and law, and setting up of institutes of politics and law.[2] Second, from 1957 to 1976, in which the "Cultural Revolution" ended, the "left" route and the "Cultural Revolution" turmoil made socialist construction suffer a serious setback, without development and adjustment of the theory of the state and law, and with only intensified contents concerning the state, revolution and class dictatorship in

1 See the *Theory of State and Law*, co-edited by Romashkin, Strogovik and Tumanov, Law Press China, 1963, p.35. This book was published in the Soviet Union in 1962.

2 Editor-in-chief ZHANG Youyu and associate editor WANG Shuwen: *Forty Years of PRC's Legal Science*, published by Shanghai People's Publishing House, 1989, pp.1-105.

the textbooks. In the two periods, the class struggle is the basis and main line of the theory of the state and law and, as an independent discipline, jurisprudence in fact had not been established. Later, between 1977 and 1982, China's jurisprudence had been restored, planned and reconstructed, with the theory of state and law in this stage gradually turning into "the basic theory of jurisprudence". For example, in the *Basic Theory of Law*,[1] co-edited by CHEN Shouyi and ZHANG Hongsheng; the *Basic Theory of Law*,[2]edited by SUN Guohua, they have begun to specifically expound theoretical issues of law, which has been to a large extent be influenced by the Soviet Union's theory of state and law.

From the point of view of China's actual evolvement, the theory of the state and law has on the whole a few characteristics as follows: first, between different theories of ancient and modern, dominated by view of historical progressivism, the theory of the state and law has placed in the antagonistic structure between the exploiting class and exploited class other legal thoughts and theories in the history, and in the antagonistic structure between the capitalism and socialism other legal thoughts and theories existing at the same time in the world, thus treating thoughts and theories differently from the theory of the state and law in a simple attitude of criticism, rejection and struggle, and cutting off in time and space dimensions the way to draw and communicate the ancient and modern knowledge of jurisprudence. Second, between theory and practice, in order to ensure its purity, the theory of the state and law has artificially been limited to text explanation for Marxist classical literature away from the space-time background, showing obvious bookishness and dogmatism, not fully based on the reality to rethink theoretical problems, nor on the promotion and development of the theory in practice, even there being misunderstanding in the interpretation of the classic literature, deviated from the basic value care and spiritual essence. Third, between

1 Editors-in-Chief CHEN Shouyi and ZHANG Hongsheng: the *Fundamentals of Science of Law*, Peking University Press, 1981.

2 Editor-in-chief SUN Guohua: the *Fundamentals of Science of Law*, Law Press. China, 1982.

ideal and reality, the theory of the state and law is that about the state and law unfolded under the large objective premise of "withering away of the state", on the one hand, the real level of "class dictatorship" makes the state and law stern struggle tools, and pays insufficient attention to the social foundation on which the state and law is based and its important social functions; on the other hand, the ideal level of "withering away of the state" makes the state and law not an important instrument to maintain the order of the state to be inherited for a long time, but an ultimately expedient thing, so that after the founding the New China there is still phenomenon of legal abuses, disruption of the state machine, with seeking for "great democracy" of "a vast orderly community" by way of "a state of chaos". Fourth, between theory and politics, the theory of the state and law has shown a strong political nature, partisanship and belligerence, the theory swayed by the politics and becoming an important part thereof, and legal aspects of academic branch and scientific thinking restrained; under the direction of the Soviet legal theories indiscriminately imitated, the creativeness of China's jurisprudence has also been restrained. However, it is different from the political theory of "taking class-fight as the principle" completely denied later that the theoretical inquiry, expressed by the theory of the state and law, into the social and historical phenomenon of the theory, as for efforts to maintain people's democracy and social justice, transcend modern capitalism, and construct the knowledge system of socialist jurisprudence, has in the later reform practice been greatly extended, and has also existed, in the form of new, academic theory discourse, in today's knowledge system of jurisprudence.

2. Succession and Acceptance by China's Jurisprudential Circle of the Soviet Union's Jurisprudential Theory

Early since the founding of the New China, abolishing the old law, and enacting the new law were the primary theoretical and practical problems. Revealing and criticizing the reactionary class nature of the old law, and interpreting the progressive class nature of the new law, became the main principal line of theoretical research of jurisprudence. In the process of the theory practice, learning, succeeding and accepting the Soviet Union's theory of jurisprudence became China's main goal and way of legal education and legal research.

2.1 Main way of succeeding and accepting the Soviet Union's theory of jurisprudence

One of the best ways of succeeding and accepting the Soviet Union's theory of jurisprudence, was personnel exchanges. In the 1950s, there were in China only four colleges of politics and law, a central cadre school of politics and law, a few university schools of law, and a law institute of Chinese Academy of Sciences. In the legal departments and law institutes, different numbers of students were sent respectively to study law in the Soviet Union. Taking as an example the law institute of Chinese Academy of Sciences then, just in the 1950s, 15 students were sent successively to the Soviet Union, who went respectively to the Lomonosov Moscow University, Leningrad University and other colleges and universities for studying theories of the state and law theory, constitution, criminal law, criminal procedure law, civil law, labor law, etc. Peking University, Renmin University of China, and Beijing Institute of Political Science invited the Soviet experts to give instruction in the three universities. Over a period of time, the Soviet Union experts of jurisprudence occupied many rostrums of the law faculties of China's universities, and teachers and professors of jurisprudence in China started an upsurge of learning from the Soviet Union experts.

Another way to succeed and accept the Soviet jurisprudence theory was the translation and publication of a large number of the Soviet Union books and textbooks on jurisprudence to make them the mainstream textbooks in Chinese law schools. In the early 1950s, Chinese jurisprudence experts and translators began to translate the Soviet law books and textbooks. The situation could be divided into two kinds: one was to translate the Soviet Union's books published in the 1930s and 40s, for example, the *Laws of Soviet States*, written by K.A. Arkhipov (Moscow, 1925); the *Soviet National Laws*, edited by A.N. Vyshinskii (Moscow, 1938); the *Theory of State and Law*, co-authored by C.A. Gronski and

M.C. Strogovik (Moscow, 1940); the *Soviet Law-Thesis Summary*, written by M.b. Zwick (Kharkov, 1952).[1] Another was the translation and introduction of a large number of the Soviet Union books and textbooks published in the 1950s and 60s, such as the *Soviet Union Land Law Course*, edited by the Ministry of Justice of the Soviet Union of All-Soviet Institute of Law (Dadong Books, 1951); the *Theory Tutorial of Marxism-Leninism about State and Legal Force*, co-authored by scientific researchers of the Soviet Academy of Sciences Institute of Law Science (China Renmin University Press, 1951); the *Theory of the State and Law*, by Denissow (Zhonghua Book Company, 1951);the *Soviet Union Constitution Tutorial*, by M.N. Kalewa, (enlarged edition, The 50's Press, 1953); the *Soviet Civil Law*, edited by C.H. Братуся (Vol. 1&2, China Renmin University Press, 1954); the *Soviet Criminal Proceedings*, authored by M.A. Челъцов(Vol. 1&2, China Renmin University Press, 1954); the *Soviet Fiscal Law*, authored by M.A. Gurwitsch (China Renmin University Press, 1954). Since 1955, China continued translating and publishing the Soviet Union books and textbooks of jurisprudence, for example, the *Theoretical Issues on State and Law*, authored by Andrei Anuarevich Vyshinskii (Law Press. China, 1955); the *Soviet Administrative Law*, C.C. Stujinikin (General, special) (China Renmin University Press, 1955); the *Soviet Labor Law*, authored by H.R. Aleksandrov (General, special) (China Renmin University Press, 1955); the *Soviet Labor Law Tutorial*, authored by H.R. Aleksandrov (General, special) (China Renmin University Press, 1955); the *Soviet Judicial System*, authored by Д.С. Карев (Law Press. China, 1955); the *Theory of State and Law*, co-authored by М.П. Карева, С.Ф. Кечекъян, С.Д. Федосефв, Г.И. Федькина (Vol. 1&2, China Renmin University Press, 1956&57); the *Soviet Inheritance Law*, co-authored byБ.С. Angemolvanov and Glavey (Law Press China, 1957); the *Soviet Foreign Trade Legal Problems*, edited by Q.M. Genkin (Law Press China, 1957); the *Soviet Constitutional History*, edited by C.C. Студеникина (China Renmin University Press, 1958);the *Theory of State and*

1 See *WU Daying Collection*, China Social Sciences Press, 2002, pp.6-8.

Law, co-edited by Romashkin, Strogovik and Туманов (Law Press China, 1963).

Jurisprudence works of the Soviet Union, and its textbooks and jurisprudence education system, have a huge impact on China's legal education. For example, in the early 1950s, the *Course Outline for Soviet Union Law School Specialized the Soviet Union*, edited by the Ministry of Justice of the Soviet Union of All-Soviet Institute of Law, was introduced into China, covering history of state and law, Soviet national law, administrative law, labor law, criminal law, criminal procedure law, civil law, land law, court organization law, etc. It should be specifically pointed out that the Cadres Training Group of Political and Legal Committee under China's Central People's Government, in September. 1954, printed and distributed the above *Course Outline* to various colleges and universities of political science and law, as reference materials to compile teaching materials and teaching outline, and as reference materials of self-study for cadres at department of politics and law. The setting up of the theoretical research on jurisprudence and teaching course in China succeeds and accepts the scope and content of the Soviet theory of state and law (including history of state and law). In addition to heavy use of the foresaid Soviet textbooks and works, notably the *Theory of State and Law*, edited by М.П. Карева (Vol. 1&2)[1], the *Theory Tutorial of Marxism-Leninism about State and Legal Force*, co-authored by the Soviet Academy of Sciences Institute of Law Science[2], and the *Criticism of Modern Bourgeois Jurisprudence Theory*, authored by A.T. Туманов[3], are all must-be-read textbooks. In 1957, the *Theory Handout on State and Legal Force* (Vol. 1&2), edited by the Teaching and Research Office of Theory on State and Legal Force of Renmin University of China Department of Law; the *Theory Handout on State and Law*[4], edited by the Teaching and Research Office of Theory on State and Law of the

1 The *Theory of State and Law*, co-authored by M. П.Карева, *et al*, and translated by LI Jaien, Vol. 1&2, China Renmin University Press, 1956&1957.

2 Published by China Renmin University Press in 1955.

3 Published by Law Press China in 1959.

4 The two handouts were published by China Renmin University Press and Law Press. China respectively in 1957.

Central Leadership Institute of Politics and Law, were compiled according to the structure and content of the *Theory of State and Law* (Vol. 1&2), authored by М.П. Кареваеt *al.*, USSR, that is, both contain in general origin and essence of state and law; history types of state and law of exploiting classes; creation and essence of socialist state, country form of proletariat dictatorship, organization structure and basic functions of socialist state; essence of socialist law; legal system, legal order and legal norm, legal origin, legal consciousness, application of legal norm, legal relation, socialist law and morality, law and communism, etc.

Soviet theory of state and law has time-honored influence on the education of law and legal theory in China. From the 1960s to the early 80s, the Soviet jurisprudence books and textbooks, in particular on theory of state and law, were still reference books for the Chinese scholars and students.

After China experienced ten years of the "Cultural Revolution" turmoil, in May 1978, the Institute of Law of Chinese Academy of Social Sciences and Peking University School of Law began respectively to admit the first year of graduate law students. Graduate students admitted by the Institute of Law included those majored in the areas of theory of state and law. Many students before the exam just referred to books like the *Theoretical Issues on State and Law*, authored by Andrei Anuarevich Vyshinskii, and the *Theory of State and Law* (Vol. 1&2), authored by М.П. Кареваеt *al.* In the *Titles and Booklist of Theory Special of State and Law,* prepared by the Institute of Law of Chinese Academy of Social Sciences, for 1978 graduate of the theory of the state and law, special subjects listed mainly included the origin and essence of state and law; state and law of the exploiting classes; theory on criticism of state and law of the bourgeois; essence and form of socialist state, and state agency; creation, development and essence of socialist law, and its formulation, application, compliance; law standard, system, legal system, as well as state and law and communism. A significant part of these theories was influenced by the Soviet state and law theory. In the *Titles and Booklist*, in addition to a list of classics of Marx, Engels, Lenin, Stalin, MAO Zedong, and DONG Biwu, there were more than ten Soviet works and textbooks of jurisprudence.

2.2 Succession and acceptance of main Soviet jurisprudence theory

China's juristic theory then succeeded and accepted the expounding in the Soviet theory of state and law on Marxism-Leninism's national and legal view. Surveying works and textbooks on the Soviet theory of state and law, we can find that they interpret such theory in reference to relevant classics of Marx, Engels, Lenin and Stalin. For instance, in accordance with relevant classics such as Engels' *The Origin of the Family, Private Property and the State*, Lenin's *The State*, and Stalin's The Foundations of Leninism, they illustrated the origin and essence of state and law, nature of state, class nature of bourgeois state and law, pointing out that in the classic works of Marxism and Leninism there are exhaustive proof: that a state "is an irreconcilable product and performance of class contradictions..." "Marxism-Leninism's national theory illuminates inalienable connections coexisting with a state between opposing class and irreconcilable class contradictions, hinting nature of state: which is an organ of "ruling class"[1], and further illustrated the nature and functions of a proletarian dictatorship state; in accordance with relevant works such as Marx and Engels' *Communist Manifesto*, Marx' *Capital, Preface to A Critique of Political Economy* and *Critique of the Gotha Programme*, Engels' *Anti Duhring* and *The Situation of British Working Class*, Lenin's *The State,* they expounded the essence of law, relationship between law and economic base, and nature of bourgeoisie law; and in accordance with relevant works such as Lenin's *The State and Revolution*, *The Present Task of Soviet's Regime*, and *Theory on "Dual" Leadership and Legal System*, they explained the essence and basic characteristics of socialist law, and the unity of socialist legal system. Furthermore, many of other Soviet works and textbooks of jurisprudence, in accordance with classics of Marxism-Leninism, illustrated other legal ideas.

China's jurisprudence theory then succeeded and accepted the jargons,

1 The *Theory of State and Law*, co-authored by M. П.Карева, *et al*, and translated by LI Jaien, China Renmin University Press, 1956, p.42.

concepts, terminologies, and definitions of Soviet jurisprudence theory. Some jargons, concepts and terminologies, and definition in works and textbooks of Soviet jurisprudence theory have been succeeded and accepted by China's jurisprudence theory, as a result of which, in the theory of state and law, as well as textbooks and works of jurisprudence theory in China since 1950s, expressions of terminologies and concepts corresponding to the foresaid jargons and concepts also drew on their contents in the Soviet works. For instance, three history types of states and laws of exploiting classes; socialist legal system and legal order; concept, structure, kind and application of socialist legal norms; concept of origin of socialist law, systematic normative documents(including codification of regulations and codes); for socialist legal relationship, its concept, main body and object, and right and legal obligation of subject(i.e., content of legal relationship); concept of the socialist legal system, and that of legal department, etc., all these words and expression are used for reference in Chinese works related to jurisprudence theory textbooks. In light of this theory transplant, micro-comparison research method can be employed to conduct the mapping studies between the two to identify the similarities and differences between the two jurisprudences.

China's jurisprudence theory then indiscriminately imitated Soviet theoretical perspectives on concept and nature of law, a theory that excessively emphasized the class nature and coercive nature of law and only regarded law as a tool for class struggle. When addressing concept and nature of law, the Soviet's jurisprudence quoted Marx and Engels' *Communist Manifesto* as in bourgeoisie "the concept of itself is a product of the relations of production and ownership of bourgeois, as your law, however, is regarded as the law of the will of your class, and the content of such will be determined by your class material living conditions"[1]. And illustrating such classic remarks, the Soviet scholars maintained

1 *The Communist Manifesto*, see *Marx and Engels' Anthology,* Vol. 1, People's Publishing House, 1972, p.268. For quotation of it in the Soviet Union's jurisprudence theory see the *Theory of State and Law*, co-authored by M. П.Карева, *et al*, and translated by LI Jaien, Vol. 1, China Renmin University Press, 1956, p.73.

on the one hand "This definition expresses briefly Marxism's concept of law (which is the only scientific one), and hinted on the other hand that "But it should be noted that this definition fails to cover all characteristics of law, but only the most important and essential ones"[1]. In this way, they left very large room, which can be arbitrarily interpreted, for their cognitive theory on concept and nature of law. Such is the case. M.П. Карева*et al.* wrote formally into the textbook the *Theory of State and Law* the definition of law proposed by Andrei Y. Vyshinsky and through group discussion at the conference by legal science workers of all-Soviet in 1938, that is, "Law, a sum total of codes (norms) of conduct subject to it, is established or approved by the state, reflects the will of the ruling class, and is safeguarded by the state coercive power to protect, consolidate and develop social relations and order benefit and suitable for the ruling class"[2]. And the scholars particularly pointed that: "In Soviet jurisprudence, the definition of law, proposed by Academician Andrei Y. Vyshinsky, is made in the light of all of the viewpoints of Marx, Engels, Lenin, Stalin and their most familiar students."[3]It was thus anointed as the "Jurisprudence theory of Marxism-Leninism" which could not be doubted. Therefore it was naturally copied by Chinese jurisprudence theory in full.

But we must recognize that such a complementary definition on law is not the original intent of authors of Marxist classics, but point of views of Andrei Y. Vyshinsky accepted and recognized in the Soviet jurisprudence theory, who laid excessive and one-sided emphasis on class nature of law, and state will and coercive nature of law, and who only saw law as a tool for class struggle and suppression, ignoring social public functions of law. This theory came in the social condition of years of Soviet violent class struggle (including the serous magnifying o "Great Purge" in the 1930s), when Andrei Y. Vyshinsky held the post of the Chief Prosecutor of Soviet's General Procuratorates, who also directly

1 See the *Theory of State and Law*, co-authored by M. П.Карева, *et al*, and translated by LI Jaien, Vol. 1, China Renmin University Press, 1956, p.74.

2 Ibid., p.75.

3 Ibid.

got involved in this kind of purging practice. China's jurisprudence then followed this theory, which caused great harm to China's jurisprudential circle and legal practice.

Due to excessively, one-sided emphasis on the class nature of law, certain inner links between old and new law were denied by the fundamental differences between the abolished old law and new law. Therefore, discussion from 1956 to 1957 in China's jurisprudence circle on theory of class and succession nature of law[1], and the discussion between 1960 and 1962 on research subject of jurisprudence and its system, should have focused on legal phenomena and its extensive social significance from more scientific view of the law and in a broader sense, yet they ended up denying the right purpose and meaning of discussion, from a perspective of one-sided class nature, coercive nature of the law, based on the theory of law being tools for class struggle. Thus the succession nature of law was denied completely, and legal scholars holding different opinions were even subjected to persecution.

2.3 Causes and assessment for succession of Soviet jurisprudence theory

The New China, under the leadership of CCP, and the Soviet Union, under the leadership of CPSU, shared same political beliefs and ideologies. The theoretical perspectives of Marxist classical writers were found throughout the books and textbooks of the Soviet Union's jurisprudence theory. Even if there were dogmatic and rigid understandings of Marxism-Leninism classics, the common beliefs and the same ideology drives Chinese jurisprudence to identify with the contents and ways of thinking in the Soviet Union's jurisprudence. Thus China's jurisprudence community naturally followed or transplanted the Soviet Union's works and viewpoints of jurisprudence theory.

In the early 1950s, in the movement to fully destroy old laws as well as fierce political struggle therewith at the beginning of the founding of New China,

1 YANG Zhaolong: the *Class Nature and Inheritance of Law,* published in *Journal of East China Politics and Law*, 1956, Issue 3.

the nature and function of law was always showing that law is the tool for class repression and struggle, fully reflecting class and coercive nature of law, manifesting the state will, so that at the time it was difficult to show the social function of law in managing the social and public affairs. In this case, in terms of direct perception of law and understanding of the theory of jurisprudence, we find consistent theoretical exposition from the Soviet Union's jurisprudence theory, which naturally aligned jurisprudence of China with that of the Soviet Union.

An analysis of traditional Chinese legal culture at a deeper level also provides a suitable legal culture foundation for the succession and acceptance of the Soviet Union's jurisprudence. Thousands of years of Chinese law was to affiliate individuals' personality and rights to a particular group, with a worship of state power and contempt for individual rights. Traditional Chinese law values public law (mainly criminal law) but neglects private law, emphasizing the authority and coercive nature of public power, while neglecting and even violating arbitrarily private rights of individuals. The Soviet jurisprudence theory emphasizes the state will of law, coercive and class nature, advocating the sanctity of public power, and ignoring the function of law to safeguard the rights of the individual and social fairness and justice, a theory in perfect accord with Chinese traditional legal culture of valuing the state but neglecting individuals.[1]

But we should objectively understand and evaluate the history in which China's jurisprudence theory succeeded and accepted the Soviet Union's jurisprudence theory. There were both internal causes under Chinese historical conditions and external causes under the Soviet historical circumstances for such transplant, with both good and bad historic lessons.

Even now, with objective analysis of works and textbooks of theory of state and law of the Soviet Union in the 1950s, the application of the principles of Marxism-Leninism classics was surely right. China's jurisprudence theory has fully succeeded and accepted theoretical perspectives supported by Marxism-Leninism

1 Foresaid viewpoints See KONG Xiaohong's *Brief View on China's Forty Year's Law Science*, published in *Chinese Journal of Law*, 1989, Issue 2.

national and legal outlook, becoming the dominant thought influencing China's jurisprudence theory for a long period of time. There is positive significance without doubt in succeeding and accepting the Soviet Union's jurisprudence, for example, the formulation of the basic structure and content for China's socialist legal outlook, the construction of the knowledge system still influencing law thinking, and the preparation of a great deal of talents in jurisprudence who played an important role later on. It should be certainly noted that, in the Soviet Union's works of theory of state and law, despite the reference to Marxism-Leninism classics, there are unavoidably some dogmatic understanding, and some principles proven to be rigid and inflexible in many ways, all of which brought serious adverse impact on China's jurisprudence in theory and practice.

3. New China's Critiques of Old Legal Views

Directed by the *Instruction on Abolishing 'Pandect of Six Laws' of Kuomintang and Determining Judicial Doctrines for Liberated Area,* issued by the Central Committee of the Communist Party of China in February 1949, New China in the early years of its founding launched a large scale campaign to destroy old legal system. An editorial *We Must Thoroughly Reform Judicial Work* on the People's Daily in August 7, 1952, clearly pointed that, "Judicial reform movement is to oppose the old legal viewpoints and to reform the whole judicial system", its purpose being on a national scale "to purify all or different levels of judiciary authorities in terms of politics, organization and ideological style", and to "establish and perfect judicial system in a scientifically proper way." Thus, the critique and fight upon and against old jurisprudence and legal ideas had been carried out nationwide.

So-called "old legal ideas" were defined by then leaders of China's political-science and-law departments as "reactionary legal ideas to rule the people that is traced to the same origin from the Northern Warlords to the kuomintang"[1], and further described by scholars as "there are many methods and styles rule and

1 PENG Zhen: Discussion on China's Political and Legal Work, Central Party Literature Press, 1922, p.70.

suppress the people, in reactionary Kuomintang's *Pandect of Six Laws* and its reactionary perspective law, including a complete set of anti-people legal system left over by reactionary rulers, from ideological system of law to organizational system of judicature"[1]. It thus appears that critique upon "old legal ideas" at initial stage of the founding of New China is in effect a total cleaning up of legal systems and thoughts of the Nanjing Kuomintang Regime.

The critiques against old legal views were in fact very extensive, which involved not just people's positions on the old law, but also people's views on the new law which may have been impacted by the old law. First, it is "Tile Theory of Old Law" and "Usefulness Theory of Old Law" that were criticized most harshly, both of which suggest that after we smashed "old construction" of law some "tiles" could be of avail to us—a view that some reasonable elements in old law may be succeeded. However, it was considered that the proponents didn't understand the fundamental differences between the people's law and old reactionary law, and didn't know that nothing good could be extracted from the old reactionary law in service of the people's judicial system, since the old law only represented the will of bureaucratic bourgeoisie and landlord class of the Kuomintang. They thus confused the boundary between the new and old law, unwittingly becoming the captive of the old law.[2] Second, such viewpoints as "the principle of that everyone is equal before the law", "freedom of contract" and "principle of the principle of non-retroactivity of law" were criticized for breaching the principle of people's democratic dictatorship and serving the interests of the people's enemy. Third, the "principle of judicial independence" maintains that "a judge should independently decide cases and shall only abide by laws". Therefore, it was against the judicial and administrative independence principle that a county chief or mayor holds a concurrent post of a chief justice/director of a court; a court director may usurp

1 LI Guangcan and LI Jianfei: *Eliminating Old View Anti-People*, published in *People's Daily*, August 22, 1952.

2 WEI Wenbo: *It is Necessary for Judicial Reform to Thoroughly Carry out Mass Line*, published in the *Reference Data Assembly for Criminal Procedure Law* (Vol. B), edited by WU Yanping, Peking University Press, 2005, p.738.

the judicial authority of a judge if the director of decides a case himself; and that it was judicial task to crack down counterrevolutionaries, which therefore should not be governed by the martial law. The argument was labeled as usurping political leadership, "asserting political independence"[1], and embodying the bourgeoisie thinking of "separation of powers" . Forth, the position that "a complete set of judicial procedure should be followed in handling a case" was considered to be out of touch with the people, causing judiciary authorities to be infected with bureaucratic style of work, and to become the lords oppressing the people. And the opinion could become an excuse to use old rigid procedures and complicated formalities to delay handling a case and suppress the people. Fifth, the argument that "the judiciary shall have its own approach and methods" maintains that judicial activities involve specialized knowledge and expertise different from political movement, and should be handled by professionals familiar with legal knowledge. The professionals adhering to judicial work approach opposed launching political movement in judicial activities, arguing that the approach of "following the masses" is a more generic approach which may not be applicable to judicial work. This idea was criticized for being out of touch with the people and the central priority of the Party and State, i.e. "handling a case behind closed doors". Sixth, the proposition of "respecting the authority of law and ruling the nation by law", was deemed as an attempt reject CCP's leadership.

Maybe it is beyond the understanding of most people today that the foresaid views which for the most part may be regarded as "legal axioms" or common sense, were attacked by the new regime in a wholesale way as "old law doctrines"? This could be answered after we carefully review the relevant history and explore possible reasons. "For a legal revolution, how to deal with its legal heritage is an important question that the architect of the revolution must give serious thoughts. Under the then historical circumstances, the Chinese Communist party acutely understood that China's socialist legal

1 YE Lan: *Eliminating Old View Anti-People*, published in *People's Daily*, October 17, 1952.

system could never be built on the old legal system, and that it was necessary to smash the old state machinery with revolutionary violent means, that is, to abolish the pseudo legal authority and legitimacy of the reactionary Kuomintang government."[1]The *Instruction on Abolishing 'Pandect of Six Laws' of Kuomintang and Determining Judicial Doctrines for Liberated Area,* issued by the Central Committee of the Communist Party of China in February 1949, conformed to the general understanding of average Communist party members, i.e., the legal system of the Kuomintang, like other bourgeoisie laws, behind hypocrisy veil of so-called "everyone being equal before the law", is in effect a tool to maintain the ruling of landlord class and bureaucratic bourgeoisie class, and a weapon to suppress and shackle the people; while the "government system of people's democratic dictatorship is the powerful weapon to guarantee the victory of the people's revolutionary achievements and to oppose restoration of a dethroned monarch by enemies at home and abroad, a weapon that we must grasp firmly"[2]. Since "political power grows out of the barrel of a gun", the Communist Party must grasp firmly the "Knife handle" of the people's democratic dictatorship so as to ensure consolidation, stabilization and development of the New Democratic society. So the basic spirit and direction of New China's legal system development was necessarily to abolish the "*Pandect of Six Laws*" to start all over again. Aimed at the proposition that quite a few judicial cadres then put forward that the reasonable parts of legal system of the kuomintang should be used in the liberated regions, the Central Committee of the Party made it clear that no part of the "*Pandect of Six Laws*" could be retained. It showed not only the determination of Communist Party to sever with the old regime, but also the self-confidence of Communist Party to build new regime in their own way.

At the early days of the New China, although the Kuomintang *'Pandect of Six Laws'* was abolished as a whole, "old law views" left by it had a broad and

1 GONG Pixiang as editor-in-chief: the *Legal Revolution of Contemporary China*, Law Press China, 1999, pp.40-41.

2 *Selected Works of MAO Zedong*, Vol. 5, People's Publishing House, 1977, p.5.

profound influence on legal community and legal education. For example, in land reform, some judicial officers treated landlords and peasants in the same way based on the principle of "all being equal before the law", declaring the strict 12 court procedural rules at the start of a hearing. Yet peasants with generally poor education were intimidated by the rules in all manners and dared not speak, while landlords with generally better education held their head high to speak with eloquence and assurance. Such judicial officers didn't understand that the people's court should safeguard the peasants' anti-feudalism fight in an orderly way to suppress landlords, and therefore were deemed to in effect help landlords. In the movement of suppressing counterrevolution, for some counterrevolutionaries doing all kinds of evil and bitterly hated by the people in the past, some court officials intentionally or unintentionally exculpated some counterrevolutionaries and mitigated their penalty pursuant to such "old law views" as "crime not accomplished", "statue of limitation" and "counterrevolution being an official act executing superiors' orders." Handling obviously unequal contracts entered into by and between rogue landlords or capitalists and the average people, some courts recognized in law the validity of such contracts in the light of such "old law doctrines" as "freedom of contract" and "private right relationship", without considering that people's courts should safeguard working people and the State's public interest in accordance with revolutionary law. All of which indicate that the "very steady" and "even-handed" judicial system and ideas mainly used in peaceful times couldn't adapt themselves at all to the development of the "violent-storm-style" revolution movement, and become powerful weapon and "knife handle" with high proficiency for the people's democratic dictatorship. After the old laws had been abolished, it seems understandable from political perspective that the aforesaid legal views and principles, seemingly perfectly neutral, were deemed as "old law viewpoints" and criticized. From today's point of view, it was obviously an improper act just as when one pours away used bath water, he throws away the bathtub together. But considering situations back then at home and abroad and the Party's political thinking and ideological doctrines, throwing away "old law viewpoints" of "bathtub" and "old law" of "used bath water" might as well be an acceptable approach to resolve the then questions in revolutionary practice.

Given the historical background back then, there were benefits to criticize "old law viewpoints" on the whole. First, a political regime built on brand new ideology nature must sweep away the old political regime, including laws and ideology attached thereto. Thus, the criticism of "old law viewpoints" in the then circumstances was an unavoidable political option. Second, the basic direction of the criticism of "old law views" was right, which exposed thoroughly the nature of the old regime and legal system of the kuomintang, and might eliminate its control over the society in legal system and legal philosophy. Third, such a thorough campaign might unify the thinking in the legal community, especially the judicial circle, which helps build a brand new judicial team so as to meet the legal system requirements during the social revolution. Forth, such criticisms facilitated the wholesale succession of the socialist legal theory (mainly the Soviet Union's jurisprudence theory) later on.

Without doubt, the judicial reform movement since 1952 with strong political agenda left behind serious consequences for the socialist legal system development later. A socialist state may need to abolish old laws, yet it does not mean that there is no common ground between the new and old law. For instance, such jurisprudence principles as "all are equal before the law", "freedom of contract", "independence of trial and adjudication", "due process", "the principle of legality in criminal law", "non-retroactivity of law", and "laws should be inherited", are "self-evident truth" or legal axioms which should be recognized in any society with rule of law. These legal "axioms" were criticized and rejected as "old law viewpoints", which shows that the new regime only emphasized the political nature of law while ignoring its professional and technical nature. If no succession between the old and new law is recognized, the new socialist legal system building would become "water without a source and a tree without roots". It is obviously dangerous that a batch of well-trained "old law" people with personal integrity and legal expertise were kicked out of the judiciary, and a group of legal experts and professionals without political problem were excluded from the new judiciary and university pulpits, whereas a lot of revolutionary cadres with poor education and barely any legal knowledge were staffed as judges, so-called the approach of judicial popularization. It may be useful for the time being, but caused great harm and damage lying ahead. In this sense, the criticism of the "old law views" in the judicial reform movement were overdone with a bit paranoia, which in fact negated the law and justice themselves. Even back then, perceptive people realized the problem. For example, DONG Biwu pointed out in his speech at the Eighth National Congress of CCP that, "At initial post-liberation period, we have launched in succession several nationwide masses movements, with performance more than expected. And such revolutionary masses movements have not very much relied on the law, which may have brought some byproduct. And the mentality of proposition that the people should look down on all of the legal systems has also increased the difficulty for the Party and State to overcome such mentality"[1]. Denying and abandoning simply and brutally all the "old law views" and "old laws" will inevitably create the historical tendency of legal nihilism.

After the basic completion of the socialist transformation of private ownership of means of production in 1956, the Chinese society entered a new stage of development. The Eighth National Congress of CCP correctly analyzed the changes to domestic class relations and the principal contradiction in the society, determining that the class contradiction was no longer the domestic principal contradiction, and that the Party's working focus should turn to the socialist economic development. Therefore, the Central Committee of CCP decided to carry out the rectification movement in the Party, calling on the people to put forward

1 *Collected Works on Jurisprudence of DONG Biwu*, Law Press. China, 2001, p.350.

criticism to the Party. Inspired by the spirit of "contention of a hundred schools of thought, and flowers of every kind being in bloom", China's jurisprudence circle was active in atmosphere, and people had ideological emancipation, carrying out a heated discussion. Which mainly involved the jurisprudence topics as follows: class character and inheritance of law, relationship between the Party and law (policies and laws), and the rule of law.

Since the Constitution was enacted in 1954, the nationwide legislative process had sped up obviously. In making a new law, it is an urgent-to-solve question whether or not to use for reference and absorb useful and reasonable elements in old laws. In 1956's *Journal of East China University of Political Science and Law*, three papers were published one by one, the *Contention of a Hundred Schools of Thought and Legal Science*, authored by LI Liang; the *Discussion on Old Law in Contention of a Hundred Schools of Thought*, by LIU Huanwen; and the *Class Nature and Inheritance of Law*, by YANG Zhaolong. Then in 1957's bimonthly of *Law Science*, biweekly of *Politics and Law*, and college journal of *Teaching and Learning* of the Central Cadre School of Politics and Law, articles on class character and inheritance of law were published one after the other. In discussion, most scholars maintained that, in the old era of there being an immense number of books, law materials had their own rich heritage, which could be absorbed and utilized upon criticizing it; but they disagreed with some views such as "the internal links between new and old law" raised by LIU Huanwen and those on class character and inheritance of law by YANG Zhaolong. In order to implement the "Double Hundred" policy, Shanghai Jurisprudence Society convened a special academic symposium on March 14, 1957, which were attended by 50 persons including faculties of East China University of Political Science and Law, Fudan University School of Law, and Shanghai Law School as well as legal personnel of Shanghai political-judicial agencies and those in the wider jurisprudence circle. The symposium discussed the following questions: relationship between law and economic base; if class character unifies or not; whether there is any inner link between new and old law, new and old law ideology and new and old jurisprudence; whether old law could be used in the socialist state; significance and scope of jurisprudence heritage.[1]The academic debate in the jurisprudence circle from 1956 to 1957 were carried out around class character and inheritance of law, embodying a concentrated reflection of the general view by the people then on the nature of law.

After the founding of New China, basic laws such as criminal law, civil law, criminal procedure law and civil procedure law were not timely enacted, with quite imperfect legal system and there being instead in juridical practice a large number of applicable Party's policies and government rules. In the first half of 1957, many people criticized the phenomenon of confusing the Party with the government, maintaining that the Party's substitution for the government and the policy for law couldn't ensure the proper hearing and trial. Focused on the discussion in the jurisprudence of the relationship between law and policy[2], somebody emphasized that it was necessary to make a clear distinction between policy and law, maintaining that policy was the concrete form of politics, and enacted by the Party under then specific circumstances, with characteristics such as transiency, principle nature and flexibility; whereas law is enacted by organs of state power through legislative procedures, which is code of conduct with stability, definitiveness and authority, and the law applicable to judicial hearing could ensure accuracy and consistency. Therefore, they argued that law should be the major instrument to govern the society, and that mature and stable parts in the Party's policies should be timely converted into law through legislative

1 See systemized by MEI Naihan: *Discussion on Class Nature and Inheritance of Law*, published in *Law Science*, 1957, Issue 2.

2 See Discussion on Class Nature and Inheritance of Law, systemized by Mei Naihan, published in Law Science, 1957, Issue 2.

3 See Zhu Enlin: Relationship Between Law and Policy, Law Science, 1957, Issue 6; Wan Shan: Brief Discussion on Relationship Between Law and Policy, Law Science, 1958, Issue 4; Gao Chengxian: Applicable Law Must be Subject to Party's Policy, Law Science, 1958, Issue 8; Guang Bo: Law Must be Subject to Party's Policy, Law Science, 1958, Issue 5; Zhao Qing: Several Questions on Law and Policy, Law Science, 1958, Issue 2; Zhang Dazhi: Policy is Soul of Law, Chinese Journal of Law, 1958, Issue 3.

procedures. Whenever there is any law, we should handle cases in accordance with such law; policy could be only used as supplementary means for law where there is no law. However, mainstream views then in China's political-legal organs and the jurisprudence circle argued that policy was higher and greater than law, the former lower than and subject to the latter; that cases should be handled in the light of policy; that law and policy should be entirely equivalent. Yet on the issue that law should be decided by policy, there was consensus among the academic circle.

After such objectives were put forward at the Eighth National Congress of CCP, as the inner-party democracy and people's democracy and strengthening of the rule by law, how to strengthen the socialist legal system construction became one of the hot-button topics studied and discussed in then jurisprudence circle. Some articles criticized the status quo of the legal system, maintaining that the problems that the legal system was incomplete and not respected were very serious, and the significance of the perfecting legal system and strengthening institutional building must be emphasized. And others directly pointed that disrespect for the legal system might endanger the people's democracy. Since class struggle was basically over, law should primarily be a weapon to protect human rights, and defend citizens' democratic rights. Therefore the socialist legal system and socialist democracy were organically consistent.

The new ideological trend in jurisprudence in 1957 deepened people's understanding of the nature of law, with some criticism and opinions having much pertinence and foresight. But unfortunately, in the "anti-rightist" movement beginning since summer of 1957, certain criticisms and opinions were characterized as slander with ulterior motives the people's democratic dictatorship, attempt to shake the Party's leadership, advocating supra-class and conspiracy for the anti-people old law to come back. Those who initiated the criticism and opinions had been put a label of the "rightists", and suffered a longtime criticism and injustice. Thus the academic room was blocked to further discuss the essence of law.

Since 1957, the influence of Party's "leftist" errors had been deepening continuously on the national political and social life. In "The great leap forward" in 1958 blew "communist wind" and "fanfares", which further affected judicial work. Then it was mistakenly thought that all counter-revolutionary and other criminal activities could be quickly eliminated, and that the judicial organs, in handling cases, no longer needed to hold its own position, or follow the legal procedures, thus so-called "one chief on behalf of three chiefs" was introduced, namely, one person acted as police chief, chief prosecutor and chief judge. "One member on behalf of three members", that is, one person acted on the duty of preliminary judge, prosecutor and judge. The two-level public security organs, procuratorial organs and people's courts in prefectures and counties in some regions once were combined into "Politics & Law Public Security Department", with some procuratorial organs combined into "Legal System Office" or "Procuratorial Office" under a public security organ, which existed in name only. In Feb. 1960, the Fifth Sessions of National Judicial Work still put forward struggle against Right deviations, proposing "Comprehensive leap" in the people's judicial work. Immediately following the Fifth Sessions, the Six Sessions put forward a slogan that "when there is a matter, we should handle the matter as per politics and law; otherwise judiciary staff should engage in production/manufacturing", and "when there is a case, it should be handled as per politics and law; otherwise judiciary staff should engage in production/manufacturing". And then the Seventh Sessions said that judicial procedures were "tedious philosophy", and handling a case in accordance with the judicial procedures was an "old law viewpoint", therefore, it was necessary to "break convention and reform". During the "Great Cultural Revolution", smashing public security organs, procuratorial organs and people's courts was the norm, with all of the organization systems, principle systems, working methods and styles of work destroyed, procuratorial organs cancelled, and China's judicial system destroyed fundamentally. During 20 years leading to the end of the "Great Cultural Revolution" in 1976, the mass movement and rehabilitating criminals through labor had become the central theme of the social life, resulting in widespread legal nihilism. Jurisprudence ended up becoming the appendage to politics, which obviated any valuable research results of jurisprudence.

During the period of over 20 years between 1949 and1976, old legal systems and old legal viewpoints were criticized and abandoned; however, new legal systems and new jurisprudence research couldn't be rebuilt along the right track. Such dislocations from excessive rejection of the past accompanied by lack of rebuilding the new was the tragedy of the era—a sad page in China's jurisprudence history.

4. The Nihilism of Law and Its Consequences

The founding of New China was not the simple and natural result from wresting political power through revolution armed forces. In effect, at the beginning of the founding of PRC, the political systems and steps of the people's regime were paid more attention. First, the Political Consultative Conference was convened, at which the *Common Programme of the Chinese People's Political Consultative Conference* was formulated, specifying the people's rights and China's political system; then the Constitution of the new state was enacted in 1954, explicitly specifying in details basic rights and duties of government agencies and citizens. Thus, there was in effect a good beginning for China's legal system with which to bring peace and stability to China; if going this political way, China might have had another vision of its legal system history. However, soon afterward, due to the enlargement of the class struggle and appearance of legal nihilism, China's process of the rule of law was interrupted seriously that the State and people suffered heavy losses.

In the second half of 1957, the struggle of "anti-rightists" was magnified seriously, followed by the "Great Leap Forward" in 1958, and by "struggle against Right deviations" in 1959, with a decade of catastrophe of the "Great Cultural Revolution" at last. Such period is a history period during which the legal nihilism arose in China and created serious consequences. During that period, China's jurisprudence and legal systems got serious setback destruction, with most of law departments and law majors cancelled, jurisprudence stagnating and falling behind. Judicature failed to develop in the direction of professionalization and legalization, and drafts modified over and over again of criminal law and civil law stopped halfway, causing that China hasn't had basic laws such as criminal law and civil law for 30 years. Although the previous principle was formally put forward of "there must be laws to go by, the laws must be observed and strictly enforced, and lawbreakers must be prosecuted", the phenomena prevailed in that period such as failure to observe the law, legislation stagnating, judicature operating in the way of strike and criticizing and struggling, and constant political movement, and even finally the smashing of public security organs, procuratorial organs and people's courts. Legal nihilism ideological trend and the phenomenon of this jurisprudence fading away and the legal system deserting were of reciprocal causation and promoted each other, a social ideological trend that becomes stronger and stronger and last for a long time.

During this history period, an ideology of legal nihilism having significant impact on the prevailing thinking in society existed in the minds of China's political leaders, and influenced strongly China's policy choice. At the enlarged meeting of the Political Bureau of the Central Committee in Beidaihe in August 1958, Mao Zedong said, if there were no law, it doesn't work. But we have our own set of laws... Since the Great Leap Forward, we all have carried out production, speaking out freely, airing views fully and writing big-character, so have not any time to violate the law. Without the masses, larcenists could not be tackled. The majority of the people can't be controlled by law, and should instead form a good habit. And an army can't be governed by military law; instead in effect the conference of 1,400 attendees manages the people. Who can remember so many articles in the civil law and criminal law? Although participating in enacting the Constitution, I can't remember its articles...Each of our decisions is law, so is a meeting. Only when he forms a habit can one abide by public order regulations... We should maintain order not relying on the civil law or criminal law, but decisions and meetings, four meetings per year.[1] That paragraph

1 Quoted from XIANG Chunyi's *Leadership of Party and Legal Construction*, published in *China Legal Science*, 1991, Issue 4.

obviously reveals an idea of social governance putting aside law and maintaining order with the help of the people and meetings. In the same year convoked was the Fourth Sessions of National Judicial Work, which criticized judicial "Right deviation", holding that judicial work "has blind faith in law, even makes law an inhibiting magic phrase for itself, fettering its motion in fighting against enemies." In connection with it, there arose, in the great leap forward of judicial work, "One chief on behalf of three chiefs", "One member on behalf of three members" and "forming one fist" for public security organs, procuratorial organs and people's courts.[1] These words and practices are concrete manifestation of legal nihilism.

Literally legal nihilism seems a question about being with/without law, however in terms of its foundation it mainly involves question about the effect and position of law in China's politics and the way in which it works. To the social phenomenon of a persistent lack of basic laws such as criminal law and civil law, legal nihilism to some extent can't be associated with the phenomenon of being "without law" or having few laws. But as a theory, legal nihilism is more than a simple question whether law is complete, and it focuses on at root negligence, contempt and disdain of law. So-called "A monk holds up an umbrella, defying heaven and having contempt for the law" shows it is not necessarily that there is "no law" in the politics of the state, but that law is not deemed as law at all, taking right for law, taking words for law, and taking internal documents, decisions, instructions, and personal view of leaders for law. In fact, even at the time when the legal nihilism prevailed, China's Constitution had objectively existed, because there was no law or policy expressly to abolish the then-existing Constitution. Even during the "the Great Cultural Revolution", more than 120 criminal cases had been sentenced.[2] And the *Several Regulations on Strengthening Public Security Work During the Proletariat's "Great Cultural Revolution"* (i.e. Six

1 See CAI Dingjian's *History and Reform—New China's Process of Construction of Legal System*, China University of Political Science and Law Press, 1999, p.97.

2 See JIANG Hua's *Supreme People's Court Work Report* at the Third Session of the Fifth National People's Congress of the People's Republic of China on September 2, 1980.

Regulations on Public Security Work), issued on January 13, 1967 and rescinded on February 17, 1979, appears in the form of "regulation" formulated by the State Council, which acted as "legal" basis for a large amount of wrongful cases. Considering the historical realities, when legal nihilism prevails, it is not true that there was not any law in the society but law was deemed as existing in formalism or as a political tool, only an "article" that may be neglected or deserted, mainly presenting as failure to observe the law, no law to follow, attaching no importance to law or no check of law on political authority, using words to outweigh law, being convicted due to words, and resorting to verbal criticisms instead of judicial procedure.

In China's history, there were theoretical trends underemphasizing law for a long period. Neither Taoism nor Confucianism had much esteem for law. In the Taoist view, "The more laws and regulations, the more thieves and robbers"; [1]Confucius once said, "Govern the people by regulations, keep order among them by chastisement, and they will flee from you, and lose all self-respect. Govern them by moral force, keep order among them by ritual, and they will keep their self-respect and come to you of their own accord."[2]But this kind of traditional cultural factor was not the main historical origin for the legal nihilism arising in China since the late 1950s. In terms of its characteristics, during the nearly 20 years between 1957 and 1976 when legal nihilism prevailed, political struggle was clearly the focus, while law was just considered and should be used as a tool to realize the class dominance. In addition, in ancient China there had appeared the proposition of "measuring the importance of matters to judge other than making the criminal law"[3], which has obvious similarities with "all the decision is law, as is the meeting" in the legal nihilism. It should be said that the legal nihilism has causal connection mainly with the Soviet Union's theory of state and law, the practice whereby law should not be used in the construction period simply because

1 *Tao Teh King.*

2 *Analects of Confucius·Regieren.*

3 *Commentary of Zuo·Zhaogong Sixth Year.*

it was not used in revolution and war period, and with the excessive concentration of power in the political system at that time. The theoretical rationales behind all of above deserve deep reflection.

First, legal nihilism originates from the theory of transition period the "revolution dictatorship of proletariat". Whether in the Soviet Union or in China, legal nihilism and political volatility once arose after the Communists seized the political power by armed forces. According to the Soviet Union's political theory, the "revolution dictatorship of proletariat" is deemed to obtain and maintain regime by violent means and not subject to any law. The theory is applicable to revolutionary period to seize political power, and seizing political power is very different from operation of law in terms of political precondition, social order and implementation means. However, after "contention of a hundred schools of thought, and flowers of every kind being in bloom" had got some political criticism, class antagonism and class struggle in China were overestimated, so that class antagonism was magnified and even absolutized, "once it is stressed, class struggle works", and "taking class conflict as the guiding principle" following with it; in the end, China was caught in the "Great Cultural Revolution Misconception" that "the Revolution continues under proletarian dictatorship". Since the State has been positioned as "revolution dictatorship of proletariat"[1], which preliminarily lays the foundation of the State's legal system for Political Consultative Conference and 1954 Constitution; but such foundation had been destroyed since 1957, which gradually led up to the social situation which abandoned the legal system in way of using "a state of chaos" for "a vast orderly community".

Second, legal nihilism and legal instrumentalism are indivisible. Law is a tool for the ruling class to rule the ruled class so as to maintain its interest, a basic opinion on law in China's theory circle in the first three decades since the founding of New China. Although it was not as abroad and profound as that in first

1 *Selected works of Deng Xiaoping*, Vol. 2, People's Publishing House, 1994, p.330.

three decades, such opinion had certain influence during the reform and opening-up period. That law is deemed as a tool for political rule and class struggle, on the one hand, causes old law and its system to be criticized throughout and denied entirely; on the other, it causes law to be mainly used as a political tool for class struggle, so that there is less attention paid to social public functions of law and its role in normalizing and restraining political power. These two aspects were very obvious in the first three decades after the founding of New China. One of *Six Regulations on Public Security Work,* issued in 1967, says "Any act is of counterrevolution, which should be punished by law, concerning mailing counter-revolutionary anonymous letters; posting and distributing leaflets of counter-revolutionary, in secret or public; writing reactionary slogans or shouting anti-china slogans so as to attack or slander the greatest leader Chairman Mao and his close comrades-in-arms, comrade Lin Biao." It typically reflects the reality of the political situation led by the legal instrumentalism, under which laws and legal system must show the loss of authority and even being dispensable due to "politics in command", namely, China's criminal law and civil law could be absent for a long term, and public security organs, procuratorial organs and people's courts also did not need to have any check and balance or division of power, and even be smashed. As you see, laws completely reduced to a tool inevitably face the destiny of being abandoned as a tool, and legal instrumentalism and legal nihilism are inseparable twin notions.

Third, legal nihilism is linked to the personality cult in political life and highly-centralized political power caused thereby. Since "criticism of anti-rash advance in 1958, and 'against Right deviations' in 1959", democratic life of the Party and the State became off normal, with patriarchal system phenomena developing constantly, such as "what I say counts", namely, deciding everything by one man's say; personality cult; and placing individuals above the organization. In the period, "rule of man" was praised highly by some Party and State leaders. As a result, "what leaders say is often deemed as 'Law'; whoever disagrees the words said by leaders will be regarded as 'breaching Law'; the words changing, 'Law' changes accordingly"[1]. In the political field personality cult was accompanied by highly centralized political power, in which case law certainly will be placed under man, and from which it is unavoidable that phenomena came up like taking words for law, abolishing law or looking down on law. Thus, it must be social realities that frequent dissensions on "rule of man and rule of law" in China's theory circle and political circle in the first three decades as of the founding of New China.[2] In 1981, *Resolution on Certain Questions in the History of Our Party Since the Founding of New China* says: "some serious deviations, arising out of the problem of relationship between leaders and party not properly resolved in the history of the international communist movement, has also had a negative effect on our Party...We fail to for historical reasons systematize and legalize the democracy within the Party and the democracy of political and social life; or in spite of laws enacted they have not their own due authority. This will provide a condition that leaves the power within the Party excessively in the hands of an individual, with Party's individual arbitrary and personality cult developing, leading to the situation whereby it was difficult for the Party and the State to prevent and curb the launching and developing of the 'Great Cultural Revolution'." This passage of quote shows the personality cult and excessive concentration of power in the political and legal field; and the connection between the legal nihilism, unregulated political power operation and political turmoil. Just because of this kind of the profound understanding of such a link, the system and law does not change with the change of leaders, or with the change of views and attention of leaders—a link that has become China's important political and legal development goals since the reform and opening up.

Last, the "Mass Democracy" is also an origin for legal nihilism, led by which the operation of political power must be irregular. It manifests not merely as personality cult in political field, but eminently as the masses' power not to be

1 *Selected works of Deng Xiaoping*, Vol. 2, People's Publishing House, 1994, p.146.

2 See *Discussion on Rule of Law and Rule of Man* edited by Edit group of *Discussion on Rule of Law and Rule of Man*, Masses Press, 1980.

controlled by law. Judging by the relationship between law and politics, legal nihilism is the inevitable result of the fact that the law was completely controlled by politics and could not restrain or regulate political power and political activities. Over nearly two decades since 1957, personal arbitrary and power of the mobilized masses had been two main political right forms which had not been effectively controlled by law, while both were closed linked during the "Great Cultural Revolution", when the legal nihilism was expressed most fully. In contrast to the state apparatus, bureaucracy and courts which may be smashed, democracy was not properly tamed and constrained by law, thereby making "great democracy" manifest as an apparent "lawlessness" of "anarchy." In terms of practice, the historical position of "revolution dictatorship of proletariat" makes the way of mobilizing the masses on a large scale in the revolution and war period to be used continually in the construction period, failing to turn in a timely manner to make the people consciously maintain and abide by law. For instance, the *Six Regulations on Public Security Work* "called on the masses to assist and supervise public security organs in fulfilling their duty", with one of the articles specifying, "Anybody spreading reactionary words with 'Great Democracy' or by other means, in general, will be fought against by the revolutionary masses. In serious cases, public security departments should, coordinated with the masses, investigate in a timely manner, and act at their own discretion, as necessary."

After the end of the "Great Cultural Revolution", articles were written to criticize the "legal nihilism"[1], and somebody summarized lessons on legal system: we should govern the nation by law, rather than by policy alone; we should adhere to "rule of law" instead of just "rule of man"; we shouldn't just launch movements without attention to legal system; and we should not indulge in legal nihilism.[2] And others pointed out that, "due to longtime distraction and destruction... by the

1 LUO Shiying: *Criticizing Legal Nihilism to Strengthen Legal Research,* published in *Chinese Journal of Law*, 1979, Issue 2.

2 CHEN Shouyi, LIU Shengping and ZHAO Zhenjiang: *China's 30 Years of Legal Construction*, published in *Chinese Journal of Law,* 1979, Issue 4.

legal nihilism, there are so many taboo areas in the jurisprudence field; and even the rule of law and democracy principles specified in China's fundamental law have become taboos, such as, 'All citizens are equal before applicable laws', 'Independent trial only by law', 'General supervision', and 'Protecting the defendant's right', and people could be convicted for expressing those opinions. There were many such taboos and blind faiths and prevalent legal nihilists...who often equated the law with politics, and set the class nature of jurisprudence against its academic nature, which threw the law into 'Cold Palace' for a long time"[1]. After the "Great Cultural Revolution", the discussions in theoretical circle on calling for strengthening the legal system as well as on class and social nature of law and policy, to a great extent, involved the reflection and criticism of legal nihilism. Such reflection and criticism of legal nihilism were eventually mirrored in the Party's policies. For example, the Communique of the Third Plenary Session of the 11th Central Committee of CCP wrote, "In order to protect people's democracy, we must strengthen the socialist legal system, institutionalize and legalize democracy so that such a system and law have stability, continuity and powerful authority, and achieve the outcome 'where there must be laws to go by, the laws must be observed and strictly enforced, and lawbreakers must be prosecuted'".

1 ZHAO Zhenjiang: *Spirits of May 4th Movement and Jurisprudence Research*, published in *Chinese Journal of Law,* 1979, Issue 1.

Chapter 2

Initial Construction of the Socialist Constitutional Jurisprudence

1. Formation of Constitutional View During the Formulation of Constitution in New China

Constitutional Jurisprudence is a discipline which takes the constitution as study subject. However, in China, the constitution in the strict sense did not exist in ancient times, accordingly, the constitutional jurisprudence is not an ancient discipline too. After the Opium Wars, the Qing Dynasty who was forced by the circumstances, began to reform the political system, and enacted *Constitutional Outline Made by the Imperial Order* on September 2, 1908, which is the first legal instrument with constitutional significance in Chinese history. With the process of constitutional reform and the change of conception, the constitutional doctrines in China have also experienced the process from emergence to development. In the late 19th century and the early 20th century, Chinese scholars began to translate and introduce a large number of Western constitutional jurisprudence works, for instance, the works written by such Western constitutional scholars as Montesquieu, Duguit, Dicey and Tatsukichi Minobe. In the process of introduction of Western constitutional doctrines, many scholars began to explore the constitutional jurisprudence research in China. In the early 20th century, SUN Yat-sen proposed the theory of "Five-Power" Constitution. The so-called "Five-Power" means an institutional model, under which the administrative power, legislative power, judicial power, supervisory power and power of examination respectively operate independently and mutually supervise and balance. In the Republic of China period, a great deal of research achievements on constitutional jurisprudence also appeared, combined with the interpretation on Mr. SUN Yat-sen's "Five-Power Constitution", as a result, a large number of works on comparative constitutional jurisprudence and constitutional jurisprudential theories were published. However, the constitutional jurisprudence which makes interpretations on the state system and form of government also closely varies with the two elements. After the founding of new China, with the abrogation of old legal genealogy and clearance of "perspectives of old laws", the inheriting relationship between the constitutional jurisprudence in early new China and the previously constitutional jurisprudence actually has been cut off. The constitutional jurisprudence of new China was established and developed on basis of the constitutional concepts and knowledge system which were shaped depending upon the Theory of State and Law of the Soviet Union. In the 1950s and 1960s, the constitutional jurisprudence of old China was rarely mentioned in terms of the theoretical relationship, except during the criticism which suffered in constitutional research and constitutional interpretation.

As a knowledge which closely related with the constitutional practice of state, the constitutional jurisprudence of early new China was started up by the authority, but not the scholars, which thrived due to the urgent need of practice, but not the deep theoretical discussion.

At the eve of the founding of new China, one of the preparations for establishing new China was drafting the Common Program of *The Chinese People's Political Consultative Conference* (hereinafter referred to as "*Common Program*"). The *Common Program* is the first relatively complete constitutional instrument with the nature of new democracy, which has provided very important legal protection for establishing fundamental policies in early new China, and for consolidating the new government controlled by the people's democratic dictatorship. It is the cornerstone and starting point of the constitutional history of the new China. From the beginning to draft to being adopted in the first plenary session of the Chinese People's Political Consultative Conference (hereinafter referred to as "CPPCC") convened on September 29, 1949, and with the development and change of the revolutionary situation in China, the *Common Program* has been both drafted and named for three times.[1] And for purpose of many major constitutional theoretical issues involved, the views of various circles have all been attentively heard and absorbed. Thus, the extensive popular support and theoretical basis have been provided for successfully promulgating the *Common Program*, and for gaining its position of interim constitution.

The *1954 Constitution* is the first constitution of the new China, and it is a socialist constitution which was organized to draft out by MAO Zedong personally. The 1954 Constitution is different from the all past constitutions with the nature of capitalism, and also distinguishes from 1936 Constitution of the Soviet Union and the constitutions of the former socialist countries in Central and Eastern Europe, which is produced on the basis of theories for building a new democratic country proposed by MAO Zedong in the new democratic revolution period, combining with the concrete and actual situation in our country after the founding of new China, and by means of extensively soliciting the views of all sectors of the society. It represents a significant Chinese characteristic. The people's congress system, which was established by 1954 Constitution, and the democratic centralism, which is the principle of organizational activities of state organs, have been accepted and inherited by the subsequent constitutions. We might say that the fundamental constitutional institutions established in 1954

1 Namely, the first draft: *Program of The Chinese People's Democratic Revolution (draft)* (February 27, 1949); the second draft: *Common Program of the New Democracy (draft)* (August 22, 1949); the third draft: *Common Program of The Chinese People's Political Consultative Conference (draft)* (September 17, 1949).

Constitution have laid a foundation for the socialist constitutional institutions in our country. Accordingly, the constitutional principles and theories followed in the process of drafting 1954 Constitution have also become the most important guidelines of the theoretical research on constitutional jurisprudence in China.

At the end of 1952, the term of the first Political Consultative Conference expired, then, the choice faced were either continuing to implement the system under which the functions and powers of state power organs were acted by the CPPCC, or letting the state power system be on the right track. The Central Committee of the Communist Party of China (hereinafter referred to as the "CPC Central Committee") held that the National People's Congress should be convened in due time, the constitution should be formulated, and the state should step in a new era for building the socialism all around. Pursuant to the provisions of the *Common Program*, during the inter session of the highest organ of state power, the Central People's Government is the highest organ for exercising the state power. For purpose of the fundamental policy and other important steps pertaining to the state-building, the CPPCC has the right to put forward proposals to the Central People's Government.[1] On December 24, 1952, the CPC Central Committee proposed to the CPPCC that the CPPCC should put forward a proposal to Central People's Government Committee for convening the national people's congress and local people's congresses at various levels in 1953 to enact constitution. In the enlarged meeting of the standing committee of the CPPCC, the proposal put forward by the CPC Central Committee has been discussed. The participants of such meeting unanimously agreed and held that the proposal for convening National People's Congress to formulate constitution was right and proper. And at the same day, the proposal for convening National People's Congress and local people's congresses at various levels was put forward to the Central People's Government, and such preparations as drafting election law and draft constitution began to be set about.

On January 13, 1953, at the 20th Session of the Central People's Government

1 See Article 13 to the *Common Program*.

Committee, the attendees have specifically discussed the issues concerning to convening the National People's Congress. ZHOU Enlai, on behalf of the CPC Central Committee, made a statement for this problem; MAO Zedong made a summary at the end of the discussion, in which he has introduced the necessity for convening the people's congress and formulating constitution. *A Resolution on Convening the National People's Congress and Local People's Congress at Various Levels* was adopted at the end of this session. Under this Resolution, the conditions for convening the National People's Congress have been in place. Pursuant to Paragraph 10, Article 7 to the *Organic Law of the General People's Government*, the local people's congress at various levels generated by universal suffrage would be widely convened in 1953, and on this basis, the National People's Congress would be held to formulate constitution. In order to draft the constitution, on January 13, 1953, the Central People's Government Committee decided to establish the Constitution Drafting Committee of the People's Republic of China, which was presided by MAO Zedong, and consisted of 33 members, to be responsible for drafting constitution. For ease of the Political Bureau to discuss the draft of constitution, pursuant to the work plan, each member of the Central Committee in Beijing should take time out of his/her busy to read reference materials concerning to constitution, the reference books include: (1) Constitution of the Soviet Union. *1936 Constitution* and Stalin's reports. (2) Constitutions of the democratic countries in East Europe. The constitutions of such countries as Romania, Poland, German Democratic Republic, and Czechoslovakia. (3) Constitutions of the old China. "Temple of Heaven" Draft Constitution (1913), CAO Kun Constitution (1923) and JIANG Jieshi Constitution (1946). (4) Constitutions of the major capitalist countries in Europe and America such as France and Germany.

After working for more than one month, the constitution drafting group finished the first draft of constitution. On February 18, the first draft was delivered to the members of the Political Bureau of Central Committee and the members of the Central Committee in Beijing. After February 20, LIU Shaoqi presided over the Political Bureau, and has discussed with the members of the Central Committee in Beijing for three times. Meanwhile, the draft was delivered to the CPPCC members for soliciting proposals. On March 8, after repeated discussions and modifications at the Enlarged Meeting of the Political Bureau of Central Committee, the work for drawing up the draft constitution basically finished, and the constitution drafting group accordingly made amendments. On March 9, the work for drawing up the draft constitution was finished by the constitution drafting group, which lasted for more than two months. On March 17, the constitution drafting group went back to Beijing. In mid-March, ZHOU Enlai and DONG Biwu invested the members of the Constitution Drafting Committee who were not Communist Party members to have a discussion on it. During this period, the Central Committee further appointed DONG Biwu, PENG Zhen and ZHANG Jichun to form research group, and asked ZHOU Gengsheng and QIAN Duansheng to serve as legal counsel, YE Shengtao and LV Shuxiang as linguistics consultant, to carry out special research on the draft constitution. Through the above efforts, the *Draft Constitution of the People's Republic of China (First Draft)* was formally established, which would be propound as proposal by the CPC Central Committee to the Constitution Drafting Committee. This draft, as the basis of discussion in the Constitution Drafting Committee and at the First Session of the First National People's Congress, has established the fundamental framework for 1954 Constitution.

Under the personal leadership of MAO Zedong, the constitution drafting group of the CPC Central Committee has played a very important role in the drafting of 1954 Constitution. In this process, MAO Zedong has not only established the general framework and compiling principles of the constitution, but also conducted repeated research and demonstration on each part of this constitution, in which many terms were determined personally by MAO Zedong. In the process of drafting constitution, MAO Zedong has read many theoretical works pertaining to constitution, and has put a great deal of efforts into the process. In the draft constitution, there were many important comments made by MAO Zedong, for example, the “statements”, in the mimeographed typoscript, on Article 5, the original text of which was “the ‘capitalist ownership’ in this Article includes rich peasants”. For the expression “includes rich peasants”, MAO Zedong commented that it was not very proper. The “all citizens” in Article 16 to the original draft was drew with two vertical lines, and the question, “what’s citizen”, was attached to. Furthermore, he marked an insert symbol after the clause which was expressed as “collude with the foreign imperialism, betray his country”, and then made such supplements as “provoke civil strife, overthrow the government”. The original draft constitution has once showed that “this is the first constitution in China”, since nine constitutions have been formulated over the past, therefore, MAO Zedong held that it was not proper, and, he told us to respect the history, but not betray. Furthermore, he emphasized that this sentence “had to be modified”.[1] Due to the prominent role played by MAO Zedong in design and enactment of 1954 Constitution, then some people proposed to name this constitution as MAO Zedong Constitution[2], but this proposal was rejected by MAO Zedong. He deemed that it was neither scientific nor reasonable. From the perspective of constitutional history, the research on 1954 Constitution must be combined with the study on MAO Zedong’s constitutional thought. The historical contributions of MAO Zedong in the constitutional practice and theory shall be objectively evaluated.

For purpose of the characteristics of 1954 Constitution, on June 14, MAO Zedong made a summary on the experience for drafting constitution in an important speech *about the Draft Constitution of the People’s Republic of China* at the 30th Session of the Central People’s Government Committee. He held that there are two main reasons for the support given by the popular to this draft constitution: first, the draft constitution has summarized the experience, second,

1 XU Qiandong: *Chief Designer of the First Constitution of New China: Anecdote about MAO Zedong in Drafting Constitution at Liu Zhuang, Over the Party History*, 1994, Issue 5.

2 *MAO Zedong: A Biography* (1949-1976), in PANG Xianzhi & JIN Chongji (eds.), Central Party Literature Press, 2003, 1st edition, p.337.

it represents the combination of principle and flexibility. After summarization on the constitutional principles, MAO Zedong concluded two principles, that are democracy and socialism. He pointed out, our constitution is a socialist constitution, the establishment of which was mainly based upon our own experience, but also with reference to the good things in constitutions of the Soviet Union and the people's democratic states. For purpose of constitution, the bourgeoisie is a foregoer. Whether Britain, France or America, all bourgeois states have experienced revolution, and the constitutions thereof were established in such periods. Therefore, we can not deny the bourgeois democracy completely, and repudiate the historical role played by such constitutions. After interpreting the principle and flexibility, MAO Zedong particularly emphasized that the constitution must be complied. He pointed out, after the constitution was adopted, all the people in our country shall comply with it, especially the staff of state organs shall take the lead to abide by it. And, non-compliance means a violation of the constitution. An organization must have a charter, and a state also needs a charter. The constitution is exactly a general charter, and a fundamental law. The initiatives of the people all over the country can be improved when using the constitution, such a fundamental law, to fix the principles of the people's democracy and socialism, and then to show the people a clear path which they believe plain, definite and correct. In his speech, MAO Zedong also especially mentioned that, the process of establishing constitution is a process of exploring science. Other than science, we shall believe nothing. That is to say, don't be superstitious. MAO Zedong's speech has correctly clarified the basic spirits of *1954 Constitution*, and has propounded the guidelines for implementing constitution. [1]

2. Constitutional Jurisprudence Based on Class Struggle Doctrine

After the founding of new China, although we have formulated the *Common Program* and *1954 Constitution*, but for quite a long time, the jurisprudential theory in our country had been strongly influenced by the jurisprudential theory

1 *MAO Zedong: A Biography* (1949-1976), in PANG Xianzhi & JIN Chongji (eds.), Central Party Literature Press, 2003, 1st edition, pp.332-334.

of the Soviet Union. And the state law theory of the Soviet Union was directly copied by many researches in China. Therefore, the theoretical exploration around constitutional theories basically was not out of the framework guided by "class struggle doctrine", with distinct characteristics of the times.

After the founding of new China in 1949, with the abrogation of the so-called "fake legal genealogy", the theoretical research on constitutional jurisprudence in our country has completely abandoned the antecedent constitutional doctrines. The constitutional jurisprudence theory which took the method of class analysis as basic method has been gradually formed in Chinese academic circle. However, it began to overwhelmingly incline toward to the state law theory of the Soviet Union, even wholly accept it without discrimination. The constitutional jurisprudence scholars in this period have translated and introduced a great number of constitutional institutions and theories of the Soviet Union. The representative works included *Critique on Bourgeois Constitution by Lenin*, written by XU Chongde[1], and *Lenin's Critique on Constitutional Views of K. Kautsky and Frank*, written by XIAO Weiyun[2]. However, the universal principles in the past constitutional theories were still unconsciously affecting the constitutional jurisprudence in our country. After all, many early constitutional jurisprudence scholars, such as QIAN Duansheng and ZHANG Youyu, had written a great deal of constitutional jurisprudence papers and monographs before the founding of new China, in which many views were based on the constitutional theories at that time. Due to the successions between the teachers and disciples, many subsequent constitutional jurisprudence scholars also, to a certain extent, have been more or less affected. Therefore, the universal principles pertaining to constitutional jurisprudence could be inherited and continued.

The method of class analysis was once the basic method for exploring

1 XU Chongde, *Critique on Bourgeois Constitution by Lenin*, *Research on Politics and Law*, 1963, Issue 4.

2 XIAO Weiyun, *Lenin's Critique on Constitutional Views of K. Kautsky and Frank*, *Research on Politics and Law*, 1964, Issue 2.

constitutional jurisprudence in our country. Hence, when expounding the constitutional issues, we often said "class", strictly discriminated the nature between socialism and capitalism, and outright criticized the constitutional institutions of Western countries. The logic of argument thereof was roughly as follows: "The bourgeoisie implement parliamentary system, bragging about itself with such bourgeois democratic principles as 'popular sovereignty', 'supremacy of parliament' and 'freedom and equality'. Under the laws of capitalist countries, the parliament is produced by election of citizens who have civil rights, which is 'an agency to express the will of citizens'. The bourgeois democratic system, compared to the hierarchy of feudal landlord class, undoubtedly is a progress. However, what the bourgeoisie overthrew the feudal landlord class just means the rule of one exploiting class was replaced by another exploiting class, which determines the bourgeois parliamentary democracy is just the democracy of bourgeoisie. The bourgeois parliamentary system is a tool of bourgeoisie for exercising dictatorship over masses of working people. However, the bourgeoisie always cover the class character of parliament, and always disguise the parliament as a representative organization of the whole people, to create smoke screen of "the democracy of all people". Based on the request of bourgeoisie, the revisionists also tout the bourgeois parliamentary democracy as pure democracy."[1] The early works pertaining to Chinese constitution always emphasized the class nature of constitution too. For instance, WANG Min has pointed out in one article: "The Chinese constitution has affirmed the political orientation of socialism construction, which is a powerful weapon for building socialism, and extremely hated by the bourgeois rightist. But today in our country, no matter who speaks out against the socialist road, or against the constitution, he will sink into a state of being isolated and bankruptcy."[2]

1 ZHANG Youyu, *Hypocrisy of the Bourgeois Parliamentary Democracy*, *The Red Flag*, 1962, Issue 13.

2 WANG Min, *Political Orientation Affirmed in Constitution Can't be Distorted: To Commemorate the Three Anniversary of the Promulgation of Constitution*, *Research on Politics and Law*, 1957, Issue 5.

The representative work, in which the method of class analysis was comprehensively and systematically introduced into the research on constitutional jurisprudence, is *Speech on Basic Knowledge of Jurisprudence*, [1]which was collectively written by ZHANG Youyu and WANG Shuwen. Before 1978, this book was one of the scarce theoretical writings which have comprehensively and systematically expounded the theoretical views of socialist jurisprudence by the jurists in our country. In this book, the key role played by "the class character of law" in jurisprudential research has been expounded in detail. In Section 2, "Nature of The Law", of the Chapter 1, "Nature, Origin and Development of the Law" of this book, the author clearly pointed out that "Law represents the will of ruling class, which is an instrument for domination of the class", the concrete connotation of which includes "Law represents the will of ruling class", "Law is the will of the ruling class who has been regarded as law" and "the will of ruling class represented by law is determined by the material living conditions of ruling class". The author emphasized that: "The above points are indispensable for us to correctly understand the class nature of law." [2] It can be said that the views concerning to class analysis on law in *Speech on Basic Knowledge of Jurisprudence* basically represents the fundamental understanding of Chinese jurisprudential scholars on the nature of law before 1978. Even for a long period of time after 1978, the method of class analysis on law still had a dominant impact on Chinese jurisprudential theory. [3]

The constitutional rights confirm and protect the fundamental value of specific society in the form of legal norms. After the founding of new China, due to the complete abrogation of old legal genealogy in politics, the thread of research on constitutional jurisprudence has presented a break to a certain extent. In our

1 ZHANG Youyu & WANG Shuwen, *Speech on Basic Knowledge of Jurisprudence*, China Youth Press, 1963, 1st Edition.

2 ZHANG Youyu & WANG Shuwen, *Speech on Basic Knowledge of Jurisprudence*, China Youth Press, 1980, 2nd Edition, pp.5-8.

3 This book was republished after 1978, which had become the basic textbook of jurisprudence and constitutional jurisprudence at the early stage of reform and opening-up.

country, the constitutional right, as a kind of legal right, was produced with the adoption of *1954 Constitution*. With the promulgation of the first constitution of new China, the constitutional right came into Chinese scholars' vision. The article, *Basic Rights and Obligations of Citizens Provided by Chinese Constitution*, which was published in 1954, on Issue 3 of *Research on Politics and Laws* by YANG Huanan, was the early writing which touching upon the constitutional right. This Article has introduced the rights clause of constitution in our country, so as to prove the legitimacy of the people's democratic dictatorship, to refute the "propaganda machine and critics in bourgeois state", and then to display "the superiority of the people's democratic regime in our country". In the few years after the new constitution was promulgated, the essays connected with constitutional rights were nearly all centered on balance of the class forces behind the fundamental rights and obligations clauses to the constitution, so as to provide grounds for the legitimacy of the regime. Such discourses were hardly a kind of academic research, to a greater extent, which were determined by the need for external propaganda. Until the eve of the "Great Cultural Revolution", most writings about constitutional rights were formulated based on method of class analysis, which had even been used in the extreme. For example, in 1962, GUAN Huai published a paper entitled as "*On Personal Ownership of Chinese Citizen*"[1], in which, although the method of class analysis was used for expounding the difference between the personal ownership of Chinese citizen and the personal ownership of capitalism, but in the meantime, the scope and the way for protecting personal ownership were also objectively analyzed. This paper was one of the scarce papers with the characteristics of academic research in then jurisprudential circle. However, with regard to GUAN Huai's paper, CHAI Fabang, starting from the perspective of class analysis, propounded a view with tit for tat. He held that there was essential difference between the personal ownership of citizen and the ownership of

1 *Research on Politics and Law*, 1962, Issue 3.

individual laborer[1]. This mechanical method of class analysis represented the political tendency of the constitutional right theory in China at that time.

During the ten years of "Great Cultural Revolution", our constitution, which has provided the fundamental rights, became "a piece of paper labeling the people's rights". The research in connection with constitutional issues, even the whole jurisprudence was basically at a standstill. In essence, the constitution has disappeared in Chinese society, and the constitutional jurisprudence also sank into isolation. At that time, for purpose of the theories and opinions concerning to constitution, it was just the "anti-constitutional jurisprudence" which presented in the form of "Four Democratic Means"[2].

Comprehensively surveying the state of theoretical research on Chinese constitutional jurisprudence for nearly 30 years from 1949 to 1978, it can be found that three different development stages as follows have emerged successively during this period[3]: the first stage (1949-1956), which was characterized by promoting and introducing the socialist constitution theories; the second stage (1957-1965), which was marked by the circuitous development of constitutional jurisprudence; the third stage (1966-1976), which was characterized by the complete desolation of the constitutional jurisprudence.

At the first stage, based on the implementation of the *Common Program* and the formulation and implementation of 1954 Constitution, with drawing lessons from the jurisprudential theories of the Soviet Union, Chinese jurists have translated and introduced a great deal of socialist constitution theories. According to incomplete statistics, from 1949 to 1956, a total of 344 kinds of constitutional

1 CHAI Fabang, *On the Essential Difference between the Personal Ownership of Citizen and the Ownership of Individual Laborer in China, Research on Politics and Law*, 1962, Issue 4.

2 Namely, the "Great Democracy" implemented by means of "free airing of views, great debates and big-character posters", which was advocated during the "Great Cultural Revolution".

3 The following materials see *A Brief Review on Constitutional Jurisprudence Research*, Tianjin Education Press, 1989, 1st Edition, pp.78-82.

books have been published, which included 206 kinds of works, and 138 kinds of materials. Meanwhile, a number of constitutional jurisprudence papers have been published. These books and papers involved general provisions of constitution, Chinese and foreign constitutional documents, Chinese and foreign constitutional histories, Chinese and foreign electoral systems, state organs, regional autonomy of minority nationalities, the fundamental rights and obligations of citizen, etc.

At the second stage, as other socialist causes, the research work on constitutional jurisprudence in our country experienced a process of circuitous development. In this period, despite the Anti-rightist Movement was enlarged in 1957, but from 1960, the CPC Central Committee decided to implement the policy of "adjustment, consolidation, enrichment and improvement" on national economy, formulated a series of correct policies and measures, and rectified the "Left" deviation mistakes in past. As a result, the economic and political situations in China took a favorable turn, and the national economy got relatively smooth recovery and improvement. Accordingly, the research on constitutional jurisprudence in our country has also made some progress. First of all, in this period, the organization and personnel specializing in research on constitutional jurisprudence emerged in China. In 1958, the Institute of Law was established under the Department of Philosophy and Social Science of Chinese Academy of Sciences. Under the Institute of Law, there were three research groups, in which the first research group was specialized in the researches on such disciplines as jurisprudential theories, constitutional jurisprudence and civil jurisprudence. Secondly, despite the research achievements obtained at this stage were not in the same class with the first stage, but there were still a certain number of writings, and some of which were with certain quality. According to incomplete statistics, in this period, a total of 78 kinds of constitutional books which included 39 kinds of works and 39 kinds of materials, and hundreds of papers have been published, which involved such issues as general provisions of constitution, Chinese and foreign constitutions, Chinese and foreign constitutional histories, the rights and obligations of citizen, Chinese and foreign judicial organs and procuratorial organs, foreign parliament and election. However, at this stage, influenced by the "Left" deviation mistakes, the quantity of constitutional jurisprudence works reduced, and the quality of which was largely affected too. Many "forbidden zones" which could not be touched upon appeared. In addition, the educational institutions with respect to constitutional jurisprudence began to reduce too. According to statistics, at the end of 1951, there were 36 law departments of universities and special political and law colleges, but by 1963, this number dropped down to 8.

At the third stage, the ten-year unrest made the socialist legal system undergone overall damage, and the research work on constitutional jurisprudence completely stopped too. In this period, there were only two law departments in the whole country, namely, the law departments of Peking University and Jilin University. The law departments of other universities, and other universities and colleges of political science and law had been revoked, and the Institute of Law of Chinese Academy of Sciences was listed as a unit to be canceled too. Most constitutional researchers and teaching staff were sent to May Seventh Cadre School to accept remodeling.

In December 1978, the bulletin issued at the 3rd Plenary Session of the 11th Central Committee of CPC showed that "The civil rights provided by constitution shall be firmly protected, no body can infringe the civil rights." For the Chinese constitutional jurisprudence circle which has undergone the turbulence caused by the "Great Cultural Revolution", such assertion in the bulletin, to a great extent, means a declaration of regeneration in politics, which not only removed the worries about researching constitutional rights, but also could guarantee the correct political orientation of the research on constitutional rights carried out by scholars. Since then, the constitutional jurisprudence scholars began attempting to carry out academic research on constitutional issues. Especially taking the amendment of 1982 Constitution as turning point, the theoretical research on constitutional jurisprudence has been constantly explored both in depth and breadth. In China, the constitutional jurisprudence has really begun to regenerate.

Chapter 3

The Branch Jurisprudence with Fragmented System Suffering Ups and Downs

1. The Criminal Jurisprudence Under the Guidance of the Theory of Class Struggle

1.1 The process of drafting the criminal law and the changes of view of the criminal law reflected from it

Research of criminal law can be divorced from the law, but if there is no a criminal law in a country, it is certain that the study of its criminal law will not be in a positive way. As some scholars pointed out: a relationship of dual interaction is shown between criminal legislation and theory of criminal law. Chinese modern criminal jurisprudence is originated from the movement of reform and law revision presided by SHEN Jiaben at the beginning of the 20th century, which proves that it is the need of criminal legislation that promoted the formation and development of Chinese modern criminal jurisprudence, in reverse, the development of criminal jurisprudence also contributed to the perfection of the criminal legislation.[1] After the establishment of new China in 1949, "Complete Book of Six Codes" in the reign of Kuomintang was abolished expressly, which had the knowledge of criminal jurisprudence attached to it deposed. Founding in breaking—China formulated some emergent one-way criminal laws and regulations in the preliminary period of the establishment of New China, such as *Regulations on Punishment to Anti-revolution in PRC* and *Provisional Regulations on Hampering the State Currency Offense* promulgated in 1951, and *Regulations on Punishing Corruption in PRC.*

Meanwhile, the preparation work of drafting a systematic criminal law was going on. From 1950 to 1954, two drafts of criminal legislation were compiled by the legal committee of that-time Central People's government. One is *Draft of Criminal Law Outline in PRC*, consisting of 157 articles in total; the other one is *Draft of Criminal Law Guidelines in PRC (the First Draft)*, a total of 76 articles. Many of who participated in the drafting work of the two drafts are legal experts, such as CHEN Jinkun, CAI Shuheng, GUANG Canli, LI Haopei, LI Zuyin etc., to some extent, the two drafts "can also be considered as their academic works" and "crystallization of their collective wisdom", and "have some blinding flash points in today's opinions".[2] But unfortunately, because of the ongoing Korean war to resist US aggression, the land reform, the suppression of counterrevolution, and the movements against "Three evils" and "Five evils" at that time, Chinese attention had not been focused on the legislation work, the two drafts mentioned above were only remained in the legal committee as two written materials, which

1 See:YAO Jianlong. *Evolution of Modern Penal Code and 'Chinese Criminal Law Theory'*, quoted in WANG Jin "*On Chinese Criminal Law Theory*", China Fangzheng Press, 2005 edition, proofreading preface. Russian scholars also pointed out: "The drafting work of Russian judicial reform and penal code in the 19th century advantageously promoted the development of Russian criminal law theory." See HE Bingsong, Komissarov et al. *Comparative Study on Theory of Crime Constitution in China and Russia*, Law Press, 2008 edition, p.443.

2 See: GAO Mingxuan, ZHAO Bingzhi. *The Evolution of The Legislation of Chinese Criminal Law*. Law Press, 2007 edition, pp.39-40.

were not arranged in the process of legislation at a time and were not submitted for public comments openly, therefore, for the drafting criminal codes in this period, we can only call it "practice writing", and see the two drafts as legislation materials.[1]

The first constitution of New China and other five organic laws such as *The Organic Law for People's Court*, *The Organic Law for People's Procuratorate*, etc were adopted at the first conference of the first National People's Congress held in September of 1954, marking that Chinese legal construction entered into a new stage, which was a great promotion on the drafting work of the criminal code. At that time the criminal code was in charge of the legal office of the Standing Committee of the National People's Congress. The legal office started to draft the criminal code in October of 1954, until November of 1956, the thirteenth edition had been drafted out. The social situation in 1956 was very good, that the three major transformation of socialism had achieved a basic victory, and the Party's Eighth Congress was very inspirational. The Party's Eighth Congress resolution pointed out clearly: "Since the socialist revolution has been basically completed, the national main task has changed from the liberation of productivity into the protection and development of the productivity, we must further strengthen the legal system of the People's Democracy—to formulate a complete legal system gradually and systematically." Under this situation, the drafting work of the criminal code was going on more smoothly, by June of 1957, the 22nd edition had been completed. After the examination and modification by the Central Legal Committee of the Communist Party of China and the Secretariat of the Central Committee and the deliberation by the Bills Committee of the National People's Congress, the manuscript was handed out to all the representatives for consultation at the fourth conference of the first session of the National People's Congress. A resolution was also made in this conference: Authorizing the NPC

1 See: GAO Mingxuan, ZHAO Bingzhi. *The Evolution of The Legislation of Chinese Criminal Law.* Law Press, 2007 edition, pp.39-40.

Standing Committee to modify the 22nd edition in accordance with the proposed opinions by the representatives of the NPC and other sections, then to announce and put into trial implementation as a draft.[1]

But the later facts showed that the criminal law draft was not published. The reason, as a scholar pointed out: "after the anti-rightist movement, the 'left' ideological tendency rose up sharply, that what was reflected in the aspects of legal work was negating laws, looking down the legal system, thinking that laws were dispensable and laws would bound hands and feet—, which stayed for three to four years, so the drafting work of the criminal code were fell into a standstill."[2]

In March of 1962, MAO Zedong pointed out on Chinese legal work: "Our country does not need only criminal law, but also civil law, and the situation now is lawless. The law is a must in our country and we need both criminal law and civil law." This directive was a great inspiration to the drafting of the criminal law. The legal office of the Standing Committee of the National People's Congress had been conducting a comprehensive revision on the 22nd edition under the coordination of the relevant departments since May of this year. After many revisions and soliciting opinions, including several conference examinations and revisions by the Central Political and Legal Committee, the 33rd edition was drafted out in October of 1963. After the review of members of the Standing Committee of the Political Bureau of the CPC Central Committee and MAO Zedong, this manuscript was also considered whether to be published, but soon the "Four-Clean-Ups" movement came, then followed by the "Cultural Revolution", so in this kind of situation, the penal code of the 33rd edition draft was eventually shelved, and "slept in the file box for 15 years".[3]

After smashing the "Gang of Four", the first conference of the 5th National

1 See: GAO Mingxuan. *Conception And Birth of The PRC's Criminal Law*. Law Press, 1981 edition, p.2.

2 See: GAO Mingxuan, ZHAO Bingzhi. *The Evolution of The Legislation Of Chinese Criminal Law*. Law Press, 2007 edition, pp.40-41.

3 See: GAO Mingxuan. *Conception and Birth of the PRC's Criminal Law*. Law Press, 1981 edition, p.3.

People's Congress held in February of 1978 was a turning point for legal work. YE Jianying, Chairman of the NPC, pointed out in "*A Report on the Revision of the Constitution*": "We still need amend and formulate variety of laws, ordinances and work regulations and rules of various aspects on the basis of the new constitution." Since then, the atmosphere of talking about democracy and legal system gradually went to warmness. Especially in a conversation in October of 1978, DENG Xiaoping put forward: "It is necessary to construct socialist legal system in our country. If there is no law, our country is messy and random. Such a situation exists in the past and the present: What leaders said is the law; Who does not approve of what leaders said is illegal and violating the law. Such a situation can not continue again." He added, "before the 'Cultural Revolution', criminal law draft had been conducted, and after several revisions, getting ready to be published. But when the 'Four Clean-Ups' came, the affairs of criminal law were put aside." Now "we need a specialized agency very much, gathering some specialists, to set out to study issues of this aspect and draft relevant laws." Soon after this conversation, the central political group held a forum on legal construction, putting forward: "to organize various aspects to collaboration" to engage in the construction of legal system. Since mid-October, a revision team on criminal law draft formed began to amend the 33rd edition of the draft, producing two editions of the draft.[1]In this process, the Communist Party of China held the Third Plenary Session of the Eleventh Central Committee with historical significance. The spirit of this conference had a great promotion to the drafting work of the penal code, and laid a solid foundation for the formal promulgation of the penal code in 1979.

From the viewpoint of criminal law, the basic views of the criminal law can include two levels: the first level is whether a state needs a criminal law for governing, the second level is what kind of a criminal law should be like when governing a country needs a criminal law. The view of criminal law of the second

1 See: GAO Mingxuan, ZHAO Bingzhi. *The Evolution of The Legislation Of Chinese Criminal Law.* Law Press, 2007 edition, pp.41-42.

level is based on the premise of the view of criminal law of the first level, that is, in the national legislative policy level, the view of criminal law of the second level has almost no practical significance when the problem of demanding criminal law or not has not been solved yet. From the drafting process of the criminal law as well as view of the criminal law and the legislative policy, it can be seen that, although 33 editions of the criminal law draft were written out, what prevented the penal code from being published is not because the specific provisions are not satisfactory in general, but the policy of whether to use a penal code or not can not be decided: firstly, the attitude of leaders to importance and necessity of the penal code was changeable, sometimes attaching great importance to and vigorously promoting it, sometimes despising and abandoning it. Secondly, in the aspect of the national policy choice, the formulation of the penal code was always relegated to a second place, as long as the social situation changed, the main task of the Party and the country would change, and then the formulation of the penal code would always be put aside. Thirdly, the criminal law was only regarded as an oppression tool of the dictatorship: when they thought the criminal law tool was handy and easy to use, the drafting of the penal code would be appealed once and strengthened for a while; when they thought the criminal law tool was cumbersome or even hampering the implementation of some more important national policies, the drafting of the penal code would be stopped and barren down. Such a view of criminal law did not only have a direct impact on the practice of criminal legislation, but seriously affected the research and practice of criminal law as well. We can see the shadow of this view of the criminal law in the major contents, discussion focus as well as in its evolution and history in this period. Because for 30 years it stayed on whether there needed a criminal law or not, while the effort of providing what kind of criminal law was in vain, even if 33 editions of the penal code were written out, it only had to wait for a long time.

1.2 The main contents of the criminal jurisprudence research in this period

The process of drafting the penal code was full of ups and downs and intermittent, but the study of criminal law was still going on in a different degree. This period was the initial period of the criminal jurisprudence study of New China, the main contents of which had distinctive start-up characteristics, which was mainly manifested as taking theory introduction as a main task, lacking of theoretical system, fluctuating by the social situation.

Firstly, introducing and studying theory of the Soviet criminal law comprehensively. On the one hand, the old law viewpoint of the exploiting classes were criticized comprehensively and denied thoroughly; on the other hand, Marxist legal theory was introduced and propagandized vigorously, and the Soviet criminal law theory was introduced comprehensively. For this reason, a group of Soviet criminal textbooks and monographs were introduced, translated and published.[1] What was worthy of being mentioned in them was "*General Theory of Criminal Constitution*", a monograph of Terra Yining, a Soviet criminal law specialist, translated into Chinese in 1958 and published by China Renmin University Press. The basic theories on criminal constitution in this book had far-reaching influence on Chinese criminal law field, which the general theory of the current four elements on criminal constitution in China originated from this.

Secondly, doing researches on some practical problems. For example, the problem of retrospective effect of the criminal law, was an issue in criminal juridical practice at that time. After the old law was denied completely, New China promulgated someone-way criminal laws, in some of which there defined the issue of retro-activity. But retro-activity was not stipulated clearly in most of one-way criminal laws, in which it was not stipulated clearly whether this law was appropriate for behaviors before it was promulgated. To this situation, there were three points of view in the criminal law academia then: firstly, the new law had retro-activity; secondly, the criminal law enhanced penalties should not apply to the previous behaviors before its promulgation in any case; thirdly, the retro-

1 See: GAO Mingxuan, ZHAO Bingzhi (editors in chief). *In The Fifty Years Of Criminal Jurisprudence In New China (Volume One)*. China Fangzheng Press, 2000 edition, p.5.

activity of Chinese criminal law should be conducted in accordance with the combination of principle and flexibility, namely, in principle it should comply with principles by the old law and of "lighter", but exceptions were possible.[1]

Thirdly, doing some researches on some relevant problems combined with the drafting of the penal code. The drafting work of the penal code was intermittent, but when it restored to draft, some problems needed researches objectively, such as the suspended death sentence system, originated from the movement of the first suppression to anti-revolution of 1951, but after playing a positive role in the socialist transformation movement, whether it should be retained continuously remained controversy in the criminal law field. "From today's viewpoint, the debate laid a solid theoretical foundation undoubtedly for the existence and improvement of the suspended death sentence system, and it also improved the development of the criminal jurisprudence research in a certain extent."[2]

Fourthly, doing warm discussions on the issues of crime and two kinds of contradictions. In 1957, Mao Zedong published an article named *On Handling of Contradictions Among the People Correctly*, then some people in the criminal law field introduced theory of two kinds of contradictions into the field of criminal law in their learning process, who thought that there existed two kinds of different-nature contradictions in phenomenon of crimes, which should be distinguished strictly in the conviction and sentencing in judicial work, resulting in a long-period debate on the issue.[3] There appeared three kinds of views then mainly: the first view was that all crimes were contradictions between ourselves and the enemy and all criminals were objects of dictatorship; the second view argued that not all crimes belonged to the contradictions between ourselves and the

1 See: GAO Mingxuan, ZHAO Bingzhi (editors in chief). *In The Fifty Years Of Criminal Jurisprudence In New China (Volume One)*. China Fangzheng Press, 2000 edition, pp.5-6.

2 See: GAO Mingxuan, ZHAO Bingzhi (editors in chief). *In The Fifty Years Of Criminal Jurisprudence In New China (Volume One)*. China Fangzheng Press, 2000 edition, p.7.

3 See: GAO Mingxuan (editor in chief). *Research Review Of Criminal Jurisprudence In New China(1949-1985)*. Henan People's Press, 1986 edition, p.24.

enemy, most of which were like this, but some of which belonged to the internal contradictions among the people; the third view was that crimes implemented by the enemy belonged to the contradictions between ourselves and the enemy, but crimes implemented by some people among our people belonged to the internal contradictions among the people. Most people held the second view, but there were debates on the standard of how to divide the two kinds of different-nature contradictions, such as theory of political attitudes, theory of the crime nature, theory of big and small anger of the people, theory of the composition of classes, and so on.[1] "This discussion on the issues of crime and the two kinds of contradictions was full of strong political flavor, but it had the profound influence on Chinese criminal law theory research."[2]

1.3 The main characteristics of the criminal jurisprudence research in this period

The jurisprudence research can not be separated from the then institutional environment, and can not get out of the then social material and cultural conditions. Therefore, the criminal jurisprudence research in this period showed the era characteristics in consonance with the social situations then, with distinctive features of the politics.

Firstly, the characteristics with a strong political color. The foregoing discussion on the issues of crime and the two kinds of contradiction was an obvious example. The discussion on the issues whether anti-revolution crime to be completed or not was another obvious example. Even more regretfully, the debate whether anti-revolution crime to be completed or not is a pure academic issue on law originally, but in a specific historical environment, it has risen actually up to a sensitive political issue. In the judicial reform movement in 1952, view of advocating to consider whether anti-revolutionary crimes to be completed began to be rebuked

1 See: GAO Mingxuan(editor in chief). *Research Review Of Criminal Jurisprudence In New China (1949-1985)*. Henan People's Press, 1985 edition, p.29.

2 See: GAO Mingxuan, ZHAO Bingzhi (editors in chief). *In The Fifty Years Of Criminal Jurisprudence In New China (Volume One)*. China Fangzheng Press, 2000 edition, p.9.

as the viewpoints of the "Six Codes" in the old China, which such a tendency of sticking a political label to academic discussion reached its peak point in the anti-rightist movement beginning from the late 1957, that whoever advocated to consider whether anti-revolutionary crimes to be completed were labeled as "the rightists". Such "simple political analysis instead of in-depth legal analysis" approach left us a bitter and profound lesson.[1]

Secondly, the characteristics with tendencies of more obvious historical nihilism and dogmatism. The criminal jurisprudence knowledge, gradually accumulated up from the late Qing Dynasty to the Republic of China, was utterly negated from the form to the content in the legal profession after the founding of new China. Whether it was the criminal classical school or the criminal positivism school, both of them were liquidated because they were subordinate to the "exploiting class".[2]At the same time, the Soviet criminal jurisprudence was carried out a comprehensive transplant. Taking crime constitution theory as an example to see, the only one influential textbook of criminal law in China published in 1957, *Handouts for General Principles of Criminal Law of PRC*, compiled by the department of criminal law of Central Cadre School of Politics and Law, published by Law Press, was basically taking the crime constitution theory in the Soviet criminal jurisprudence as a reference book.[3]

Thirdly, the criminal jurisprudence research from the beginning soon to the depression. The period between October of 1949 and the first half of 1957 was called the initial stage of the criminal jurisprudence in New China by Chinese criminal academia, when the works published was "though very immature",

1 GAO Mingxuan, ZHAO Bingzhi (editors in chief). *In The Fifty Years Of Criminal Jurisprudence In New China (Volume One)*. China Fangzheng Press, 2000 edition, pp.7-9.

2 See: CHE Hao. *Incomplete Circulation: "Criminal Theory System" In the Expansion In Chinese Modern History. The Political Science and Law Tribune*, 2006, Issue 3.

3 See: CHEN Xingliang. *Criminal Law Knowledge*. China Renmin University Press, 2007 edition, Preface.

"an extremely important period in the history of the new Chinese criminal jurisprudence, and it laid the foundation for the later development of the criminal jurisprudence"[1]. However, since the second half of 1957, with the expansion of the anti-rightist struggle, the criminal jurisprudence research began to a snub[2], till the breaking out of the "Cultural Revolution" in 1966, the research of criminal jurisprudence went into a stagnant, reversal period, and lasting to the end of the "Cultural Revolution"."In continuous political movements and social unrest, the criminal jurisprudence research went to depression gradually from the first ten years (1957-1966), resulting there being few works, to the dormant and full stop in the last ten years (1966-1976)."[3]After the anti-rightist struggle, the legal nihilism prevailed, resulting in a situation that people dare not study or mention some important theories of criminal law, such as the basic principles of criminal law, crime constitution, and so on. Teaching materials compiled in variety of schools were mostly the product adapting to the need for a political campaign, which emphasized politics too much, and the professional content was greatly compressed.[4]In this situation, not only were some principles of criminal law with obvious tags of western criminal law like "the principle of legality" regarded as the "rightist" reactionary speech, but also the crime constitution theory introduced from Soviet Union was put into limbo, becoming a political taboo. As out pointed some scholars, the word of "crime constitution" could not be mentioned again, and variety of crime constitution elements could not be analyzed, that

1 See: GAO Mingxuan, ZHAO Bingzhi (editors in chief). *In The Fifty Years Of Criminal Jurisprudence In New China (Volume One)*. China Fangzheng Press, 2000 edition, pp.4-5.

2 However, *On Complicit* by LI Guangcan published by Law Press in September 1957 is an exception. This book is deemed to enhance criminal law theoretical study level in this field.

3 See: GAO Mingxuan, ZHAO Bingzhi (editors in chief). *In The Fifty Years Of Criminal Jurisprudence In New China (Volume One)*. China Fangzheng Press, 2000 edition, p.8.

4 See: GAO Mingxuan, ZHAO Bingzhi (editors in chief). *In The Fifty Years Of Criminal Jurisprudence In New China (Volume One)*. China Fangzheng Press, 2000 edition, p.8.

crime was a unity of subjective and objective must not be taught, and so on.[1] For example, in the book of *The Criminal Law Is a Tool of Dictatorship of the Proletariat* by the criminal law teaching and research office of law department of Chinese Renmin University published in 1958, a word was not mentioned about crime constitution in the description on how to identify a crime.[2] Such situation lasted till 1976, for example, the book of "*Handouts for Criminal Policy*"(for discussion), compiled by the criminal law teaching and research office of law department of Peking University, which was namely a handout for criminal policy, but actually a handout for criminal law, in which, under the title of how to identify a crime correctly, it did not omit only the word of "crime constitution", but it emphasized to identify the defendant's origin, class composition, consistent political performance, and so on, and focused on taking class struggle as the key link, adhering to the party's basic line, using view of class struggle and method of class analysis to analyze and solve problems in the determination of a crime.[3]

2. The Socialist Transformation of Civil Law

In November of 1949, the poet HU Feng published a group of passionate poems named as *The Time Began*. But for the fate of new Chinese civil jurisprudence, the starting time should have been even earlier: in February of 1949, the Central Committee of the Communist Party of China expressly abolished "Complete Book of Six Codes" of Kuomintang. Now that the "old law" was abolished, a set of knowledge system relying on it was gone. Since the old legal world was overthrown, the new jurisprudence world must be constructed in accordance with the politics, economics, culture and even diplomacy of the new society. But before

1 See: YANG Chunxi, et al. *Generality Of Criminal Law*. Peking University Press, 1981 edition, p.108.

2 See: The criminal law teaching and research office of law department of Renmin University of China. *The Criminal Law Is A Tool Of Dictatorship Of The Proletariat*. China Renmin University Press, 1958 edition, p.20.

3 See: The criminal law teaching and research office of law department of Peking University. *Handouts for Criminal Policy* (for discussion), internally printed and issued in December of 1976, p.118.

1978, the situation of civil law could be described as: the old world had died, but the new world was unable to be born. Nevertheless, the older generation of jurists still started the difficult transition of Chinese civil jurisprudence in such a hard and arduous political climate.

2.1 The history paradigm of the transition of civil jurisprudence

After the old law was abolished, all of the civil law textbooks before 1949 were discarded, so the main paradigm of civil law was originated from the Soviet Union. The Soviet civil law textbooks were adopted directly in jurisprudence education and the Soviet experts were invited to teach directly. After adjusting departments and schools, in Law Department of Chinese Renmin University, the central cadre school of politics and law, Beijing Institute of political science and law, Southwest Institute of political science and law, Northwest Institute of politics and law, East China Institute of politics and law, the main course teachers were experts from the Soviet Union, and the textbooks were from the Soviet Union. [1] *The Basic Problems of Civil Law of PRC* (1958 edition, Law Press) compiled by the central cadre school of politics and law in 1957 was the first civil law textbook published in new China, basically with reference to the Soviet civil law theory, till replaced by "civil policy" by 1960s.

During this period, a large number of Soviet civil law works were translated into the academia of civil law, such as *Russian Civil Code* (translated by ZHENG Hua, 1956 edition of Law Press), JeKing, Bula Doshi in chief: *Soviet Civil Law* (translated by LI Guangmo et al, 1956 edition of Law Press), Bula Doshi in chief: *Soviet Civil Law* (translated by the teaching and research office for civil law of Chinese Renmin University, 1955 edition of Chinese Renmin University Press), KeyiLilloVa: *Soviet Civil Law* (1957 edition of Law Press), VeeNegiKotov: *Protection to Socialist Property in Soviet Civil Law* (translated by XIE Huaishi & LI Wei, 1957 edition of Law Press), AnGilmounof, Grawe: *Soviet Inheritance*

1 See: HE Qinhua, LI Xiuqing. *Foreign Law and Chinese Law—Reflection on China's Transplantation of Foreign Law in the 20th Century*. China University of Politic Science and Law Press, 2003 edition, pp.25-26.

Law (translated by LI Guangmo et al, 1957 edition of Law Press), AnGilmounof et al: *Branch Theory of Debt, RIGHT and LAW (on SEVERAL DEBTS)* (translated by WANG Mingyi et al, 1957 edition of Chinese Renmin University Press), and so on.

China inheriting and following the Soviet civil law and the Soviet civil jurisprudence in 1950s was related to many historical factors, such as New China then was facing "blockade" from those capitalism countries, so it had to adopt the diplomatic policy of "one-side inclination"; And it translated works of Soviet civil law and civil jurisprudence in a large scale and invited Soviet experts to China to introduce the Soviet civil legislative experience and teach in various legal departments, as well as send students to study laws in the Soviet Union, etc. But the most fundamental reason was that China had transplanted the Soviet Union's planned economic system based on a single public ownership.[1]At that time, the similarity between Chinese and the Soviet Union's national ruling method and ideology resulted in the situation that the civil jurisprudence of the two countries also adopted a similar system.

While adopting the Soviet mode, a critique was launched on the bourgeois civil law in the civil law academia. Such as for the classical texts of the modern civil law—the three principles of the modern civil law laid by the French civil code of law, the civil law scholars then carried out a fierce critique. They thought the principle of freedom of contract was just a despicable means used to cover up the economic oppression to the workers by bourgeoisie, which was a bourgeois freedom of exploitation, not a real freedom for the working people and a mask for exploitation everywhere for the working people.[2] What was interesting that, the freedom of contract was the core principle of civil law, and that they negated the freedom of contract meant the denial of civil law, so the civil law scholars did not completely

1 See: LIANG Huixing. *History Review and Prospect Of Chinese Civil Jurisprudence.* Wangjiang Law, Issue 1, Law Press, 2007 edition, p.10.

2 See: Li Haopei. *Preliminary Criticism Of Napoleon Code. Research of Politics and Law*, Issue 2, 1955.

deny the principle. It was advocated in the common textbooks at that time that volunteerism and rationality were the main principles of contract in China, but meanwhile they especially focused that there existed differences in essence between socialist rationality principle and capitalist contract freedom principle.[1]

In this period, the nadir of civil law was also closely related to the court's trial. In 1957, the Supreme People's court received 2448 new cases, together with 125 in-completed cases from 1956, in a total of 2573 pieces, in which 2545 were for criminal cases(including appeals, judicial review of death sentence, retrials, protests, arraignments), 28 for civil cases (including appeals, retrials, arraignments). A total of 2203 pieces of the cases were closed, in which 2184 for the criminal and 19 for the civil.[2] A report made by the research office of the Supreme People's court in 1957 also pointed out, after the agricultural cooperation, the land belonged to the collectives, the disputes about land decreased rapidly. The number of the national preliminary hearings on land disputes was 6070 in 1956, down 76.8% compared to 1955's. Land disputes between individuals had been eradicated by and large. These figures showed that the civil cases tried by the that-time courts were few, because the law mainly as a tool was used for fighting against the enemy of the people. In addition, the people's courts at all levels had setting of the civil adjudication tribunal and classification of civil cases, but civil adjudication tribunals heard civil cases in accordance with "civil trial policy", such as the Supreme People's Court "*On several Issues in the Implementation of Civil Policy (Revised Draft)*" (August 28, 1963).[3]

2.2 The influence of Soviet civil jurisprudence on Chinese civil jurisprudence

In this period, the influence of Soviet civil jurisprudence on Chinese civil

1 See: The civil law teaching and research office of the central cadre school of politics and law (compiler): *Basic Issues Of The Civil Law Of PRC*. Law Press, 1958 edition, pp.202-205.

2 See Working Report of the Supreme People's Court by DONG Biwu in 1958.

3 See the former quotation: LIANG Huixing. *History Review and Prospect Of Chinese Civil Jurisprudence*. *Wangjiang Law*, Issue 1, Law Press, 2007 edition, p.10.

jurisprudence was comprehensive and thorough, which could be seen the figure of the Soviet civil law in all levels and all aspects of the civil jurisprudence system.

The influence of the Soviet civil jurisprudence on the concept of Chinese civil law was prominently reflected in the following aspects: First, it did not admit the distinction between public law and private law, taking the civil law as a public law. Lenin stated clearly about this situation: "We do not recognize any of 'private law', in our view, everything in the economic field belongs to public law, not in the scope of private law."Civil law and public law were the products of class struggle, so the civil right was not a private right, but the right of the public law in essence. This influence was very profound, because of this, the civil rights could not be fully recognized and protected by the law in China, and the enjoyment and implementation of the civil rights must be absolutely subject to public interest. The civil law could not be viewed as the basic law of the civil rights society or the civil law society, so it could only be regarded as the basic law of the public power society—a branch law of the Constitution. Second, the Soviet civil law negated Party Autonomy Principle, trying to compress the space of autonomy of civil subject as far as possible. It was thought in the Soviet jurisprudence that all the people's fundamental interests were highly consistent under the socialist condition, so the ruling party could represent the requirements of the public, and the law could not emphasize on autonomy of will so much. Not only the application of property rights could not claim autonomy of will, but also sometimes the personal rights could not be conducted in accordance with the Party Autonomy Principle, either. Third, the legal policy of the former Soviet Union emphasized the role of political propaganda and education of civil code legislation, and ignored the technology and quality of legislation. This influence has been existing still to now, and the formulation of Chinese civil law is still taking "extensive rather than meticulous", "brief rather than intricate", "developing the new from the matured", "legal language as little as possible in legislation" as the guiding ideology. Under the guiding ideology, the quality of legislation of civil law was very difficult to improve in essence.[1]

The Soviet jurisprudence also had a significant impact on China's civil law system. The "*Russian Civil Code*" issued in 1922 separated the relations of land, labor, marriage and family, and so on from the traditional civil law of continental laws, then to adjust the relations with *Land Code*, *Labor Code*, *Marriage and Family Code* and such special laws. The Soviet civil code did not include the contents of the marriage law, but it included the contents of the inheritance law.[2]At that time, the civil law scholars had a dispute on whether to admit the inheritance right in Chinese law circle, but the inheritance system was retained eventually,[3] which remained the dispute of the scope and order of the inheritors.[4]The rationality of this approach was difficult to explain in theory. In 1950, China promulgated the first marriage law, which made the marriage and family relations out of the scope of the civil law.

One of the characteristics of the Soviet Law was the theory of the adjustment range of the civil law. There were no express regulations on objects of adjustment of the civil law in *Russian Civil Code* in 1922, but in which it was only provided that land relations, employment relations, family relations could be adjusted on their special codes. In 1950s, the Soviet scholars had not reached a finalized argument in the discussion on objects of adjustment of the civil law, but generally speaking, the civil law was mainly used for adjusting property relations, and also for adjusting personal non property relations in connection with property

1 See: SUN Xianzhong. *A Review on The Effects of Adopted Western Civil Law In Modem China. China Legal Science*, Issue 3, 2006.

2 See: The civil law research office of Institute of Jurisprudence of Chinese Academy of Social Science. *Russian Civil Code*. China Social Science Press, the 1st edition, 1980.

3 See: YOU Sheng. *The Significance of Civil Inheritance Law In Chinese Transition Period. Research of Politics and Law*, the 5th edition.

4 See: WU Jiandou, CHEN Degui, LI Wencai. *On The Scope And Order Of Legal Inheritors In Chinese Inheritance Problems. Jurisprudence*, Issue 1, 1956; See: GUO Sheng. *Discussion on Two Problems In The Scope And Order Of Legal Inheritors. Jurisprudence*, Issue 1, 1957.

relations.[1] The theory of Soviet civil law had a great influence on Chinese civil jurisprudence. A set of argumentative articles on adjustment objects of the civil law were published in *Research of Politics and Law* between 1956 and 1957. The focus of the debates was the nature of the property relations adjusted by civil law, but these views were obviously simple use of Marxism views on economic foundation and superstructure, and they were not really involved in the legal technology to discuss this problem. For instance, one view argued that the property relation belonged to the category of superstructure, so what the civil law adjusts was the property law relation; another view put forward that the property relation belonged to the category of the economic foundation, so what the civil law adjusts was the production relation.[2] In that-time unified textbook *The Basic Issues of the Civil Law of PRC*, it made clear that the civil law mainly adjusted other than the property relation, but also a certain personal non property relationship as well.[3]This kind of theoretical view and expressive method, with the restriction of "a certain" to describe the adjustment objects of the civil law, had a profound influence on the development of Chinese civil law academia.

The Soviet civil law had great influence on Chinese civil system, which was mainly embodied as follows: (1) on the civil subjects. *Russian Civil Code* had confirmed essentially the "citizen" instead of the natural person. The subjects of civil law were the state, the collective and the citizen, not the "natural person and legal person" in the traditional civil law. In essence, this was a thorough criticism

1 See: editorial Office of "*Soviet STATE and LAW*". *Summary For The Discussion On Soviet Civil Law Objects. Renditions of Politics and Law*, the Founding Issue, 1956.

2 Such as: HUANG Sheji, ZHUO Ping. *Issues of Property Relations In Civil Law Objects. Research of Politics and Law*, Issue 2, 1956; LI Fenwu: Is Property Relationship Adjusted In Civil Law Physical Relationship? ZHI Min, ZHEN Han: *The Main Objects of Civil Law: Several Problems of Property Relationship*; GUO Shoukang, TONG Rou: *On Objects Adjusted By The Civil Law*: *Several Problems Of Property Relationship*; all published in *Research of Politics and Law*, Issue 3, 1956. SUN Yaming, SHI Huaibi. *Preliminary Views On Civil Law Adjustment Objects. Research of Politics and Law*, Issue 1, 1957.

3 See: The civil law teaching and research office of the central cadre school of politics and law (compiler): *Basic Issues of The Civil Law Of PRC. Law Press*, 1958 edition, p.20.

of the Soviet civil law on the traditional civil law, which was because the natural person and the legal person had the spirit of the natural equality, and the Soviet civil law was to deny the spirit of equality and voluntary. In accordance with the rules of public ownership in the Soviet civil law, the subjects in the socialist civil law confirmed were the state, the collective and the individual. The significance of this division lies in the distinction between their identities and the intensity of legal protection. It is certain that the subjects the Soviet civil law are not the natural person or the legal person in the sense of modern civil law. After the establishment of the civil law system in accordance with this, such had essential nuisance on the civil law playing its role.[1] This approach has been existing till the establishment of Chinese "*General Rules of the Civil Law*" in 1986, and then it had been corrected after the adoption of "Contract Law" in 1999. (2) on the legal act system. The Soviet Union law did not use the concept of legal act, but use the concept of "civil legal act", trying to suppress the meaning expression theory representing the essence of modern civil law, and compressed and simplified it to the extreme. This concept restricted not only the application of personal meaning in property relations, even the function of personal meaning in relatives and family relations, and permitted the government to implement powerful administrative management on kinship, and tried to compress the scope of relatives.[2] (3) on real right system. Classification on ownership in the Soviet civil law completely deduced from the different forms of ownership, so where there was what kind of possession system, there was a "corresponding ownership", then correspondingly, the possession system on the foundation of the socialist public ownership had three kinds of ownership: the state ownership, the cooperative and collective farm ownership and individual ownership.[3] The Soviet civil jurisprudence emphasized

1 See: SUN Xianzhong. *A Review On The Effects of Adopted Western Civil Law in Modem China. China Legal Science*, Issue 3, 2006.

2 See: SUN Xianzhong. *A Review On The Effects of Adopted Western Civil Law in Modem China. China Legal Science*, Issue 3, 2006.

3 See: LI Xiuqing. *On Transplantation of Soviet Civil Law Model in China. Chinese Social Science*, Issue 5, 2002.

that the so-called "theory of public ownership implementation stage" divided the social persons and their rights into three levels of the state, the collective and the individual, and gave them different political status and legal protection, in which the status of the state ownership was top and the status of the individual ownership was the lowest. The Soviet civil law emphasizing the status of the state ownership and the special protection to it influenced the basic theory on ownership in China in 1950s.[1] For example, emphasizing the unity of the state ownership: the People's Republic of China was the only subject of state ownership; the object of state ownership had infinite range, if state property was illegally occupied by other subjects, the state exercising the right to request the return would not be subjected to the statute limits; if state property was illegally occupied by other subjects, no matter whether the occupier had faults, and no matter how the occupier occupied it, the state might request the return; if there rose up disputes on property ownership between the state and other subjects, and the ownership could not be determined in fact, the ownership would be presumed to be owned by the state.[2]In particular, the Soviet civil law did not recognize the real right system, and only recognized the ownership system, which considered that other real rights besides ownership were a peculiar phenomenon under the private ownership, which was introduced into China in the early 1950s. The greater influential Soviet civil law translation works in China at that time expounded only ownership, but rarely involving other rights.[3] This view also affected Chinese civil jurisprudence. China did not adopt the concept of "real right" until the promulgation of the real right law in 2007. (4) on the contract system. The Soviet contract system, on the one hand, was taking the planned decree as the occurrence basis of debt, in which

1 See: LI Xiuqing. *On Transplantation of Soviet Civil Law Model in China. Chinese Social Science*, Issue 5, 2002.

2 See: The civil law teaching and research office of the central cadre school of politics and law (compiler): *Basic Issues of The Civil Law of PRC. Law Press*, 1958 edition, pp.135-141.

3 See: LI Xiuqing. *On Transplantation of Soviet Civil Law Model in China. Chinese Social Science*, Issue 5, 2002.

the planned contract occupied an important position; and on the other hand, it was in emphasizing the actual performance of contract. Soviet scholars believed that in socialist society, debt was set for completing the national economic plan, guaranteeing the socialist property and personal property, meeting the need of the citizens' material and cultural life, and other aspects. Non performance of debt was meant to hinder the realization of the national task produced by them, which would lead that the legitimate interests and needs of citizens could not be met.[1]At that time, the mainstream view of the Chinese civil law academia influenced by this also believed that the main function of debt was to strengthen the economic ties between the socialist organizations, and to realize the national economic plan. Plan was the basis and foundation of making contract, and the contract were the means and the specific form to achieve the plan. The contract was the tool of connecting various economic organizations under the premise of executing the national economic plan, which could make the national economic plan specific and precise and played a supervisory role from bottom to top to the national economic plan.[2]

But the civil law jurisprudence was not just following the civil law of the Soviet Union and the rest were "ten thousand horses silenced". Some scholars also tried to restore some systems that could hardly be tolerated for socialism, such as the acquisitive prescription system, which was the traditional important issue studied in the civil law academia in our country since 1949.Because the legislation of Socialist countries like Bulgaria and Czechoslovak admitted the acquisitive prescription system, scholars in our country also proposed we should stipulate the acquisitive prescription system, but put forward at the same time

1 See: LI Xiuqing. *On Transplantation of Soviet Civil Law Model in China. Chinese Social Science*, Issue 5, 2002.

2 See: TONG Rou, HU Jinshu. *Consolidating Contract Discipline and Fighting For Achieving the National Economic Plan. Research of Politics and Law*, Issue 1, 1956. From the title of this article, it can be seen that strategy of explaining legitimacy of traditional civil law system was about to link with socialist ideology and popular slogans together to explain that civil law was conducive to achieving the goal of state.

that, only possession in good faith was the most basic and overriding conditions, but the approach the capitalist countries stipulated both possession in good faith and malicious possession together into the acquisitive prescription was the mercenary product of bourgeois.[1] Article 37 of the initial draft of the ownership chapter of Chinese civil law draft in 1955 stipulated: ownership shall be attained in accordance with contract, aging, inheritance, bequest and methods provided by other laws. The draft indicated clearly that the reference materials of this article is Article 77 of *Bulgaria Property Law*.

Since 1963 and 1964, *Civil Jurisprudence* as a legal education professional basic course was renamed *Civil Policy Science*, adopting the self-designed *Civil Policy Science textbooks* in variety of schools. During the "Cultural Revolution", the whole nation was thrown into anarchy that, all universities were closed including the Institute of political science and law, and legal teachers and researchers including civil law scholars were driven to the "May Seventh Cadre Schools" to receive ideological remolding, which drove the civil law legislation in China, judicature and teaching into a decade-long "stagnation period".[2]

2.3 Civil law viewpoint shown in the process of drafting civil law

In this period, what China adopted is a highly centralized planned economic system, but the contract can not be completely replaced by the plan, so the norms of contract in our country has been existing there. In September of 1950, the Government Administration Council announced the first contract regulation in China, namely, *Interim Measures of Contract Signature for Organs, State-owned Enterprises and Cooperatives*, in which it provided the kinds of contracts, and it also provided that: they shall sign a contract if important business acts between organs, state-owned enterprises, cooperatives can not be cleared immediately; the contract shall be signed by legal persons rather than individuals; the contract

1 See: ZHANG Dingfu. *Problem of Acquisitive Prescription in Prescription System. Research of Politics and Law*, Issue 2, 1956.

2 See: LIANG Huixing. History Review and Prospect of Chinese Civil Jurisprudence. Wangjiang Law, Issue 1, *Law Press*, 2007 edition.

shall be settled through banks; the contract after signing shall report to the higher authorities; A dispute due to a contract shall be handled by the higher authorities, if invalid, then parties may prosecute it to the People's Courts, and so on. This code was the basis of Chinese economic contract system at that time.[1] Since then, China also promulgated some important regulatory documents related to the contract.

In 1954, the Standing Committee of the National People's Congress established a working group led by Wang Ming, director of the legal committee, to organize the drafting of *The Civil Code of the People's Republic of China*. General Office of the Standing Committee of the National People's Congress compiled and printed *Decomposition Materials Compilation of the Civil Law of Variety of Countries* in 1955, which was originated from *Soviet Civil Code, Czechoslovakia Civil Code, Civil Decree of Bulgarian People's Republic, French Civil Code, German Civil Code* as well as *the Civil Law of the Republic of China*, and so on, which was divided into 4 series: the general principles section, the property right section, the debt section and the inheritance section. Civil law scholars participated greatly in the drafting work. For example, in the process of drafting the contract for the sale, only for the Fifth Draft, it had ever solicited views and suggestions to civil law teaching and research offices of 4 Institutes of political science and law in Southwest, South Central, East China, Beijing, civil law teaching and research offices of 9 law departments of universities like Renmin University of China, Beijing University, Fudan University, etc, as well as other 30 units.[2] The *Civil Law (Draft)* was completed in December of 1956.The draft included the general principles, ownership, debt and inheritance, a total of 5 parts, 525 articles. The draft was mainly affected by the Soviet civil legislation, especially the influence of the 1922 *Russian Civil Code*. But the following political movements like "Rectification", "Anti-rightist", etc put the draft to death. But this legislative

1 See: XIE Huaishi. *New Chinese Contract System and Contract Law. Jurisprudence Research*, Issue 4, 1988.

2 See: LI Xiuqing. *On Transplantation of Soviet Civil Law Model in China. Chinese Social Science*, Issue 5, 2002.

activity is the landmark event of our country's civil legislation on earth, marking the actual expansion of the civil legislation with the socialist nature in our country.

In 1962, MAO Zedong made a directive: "Our country does not need only criminal law, but also civil law, and the situation now is lawless. The law is a must in our country and we need both criminal law and civil law."In accordance with this directive, the National People's Congress formed a working team led by SUN Yaming, director of the Institute of Jurisprudence of the Chinese Academy of Sciences, to draft the civil code for the second time. In July of 1964, the team compiled *The Civil Law of the People's Republic of China (Draft)*, a total of 3 parts, 24 chapters, 262 articles. Compared with the first draft, drafters designed a framework: "General Principles" for the first part, "Ownership of Property" for the second part and "Circulation of Property". The draft concentrated to embody the centralized administrative economic system and the "left" economic thoughts. In the guiding ideology, the draft tried to get rid of the Soviet model, and also tried to draw a demarcation line completely with the civil law of the capitalist countries. The draft excluded systems of kinship, inheritance, and so on, but it brought systems of budget, tax and others into the code. What also need mentioning is that the language in the civil code draft had strong political color, rather than using terms of the traditional civil law, but was full of political slogans such as "holding the three red flags high", "political work is the lifeline of all economic work", and so on. Even if the civil law was drafted so as to seek political correctness, it was interrupted by the "socialist education movement" that began in 1964.

Since 1964, the legislation and research activities of Chinese civil law had been thrown into the lowest nadir since the beginning of the twentieth century, and it lasted for 15 years.

3. Science of Marriage and Family Law Becoming an Era Exception

3.1 The situation of the system making science of marriage and family law become an independent discipline

In the 60 years, Chinese marriage and family jurisprudence research has been closely related to development periods of the economic society, and closely connected with activities of the national legislation. Chinese marriage and family law science discipline established in the 1950s has gained boundless vitality and vigor with the transformation of social institution and the change of the people's concept on marriage and family in the 30 years since 1978 after crossing the stagnation period between the mid 1960s and the mid 1970s. Reviewing the bumpy legal history and the tasting-hardship jurisprudence history compared with social treatment of civil law and other department laws and historical circumstances of science of civil law and other department law sciences since the founding of the new China, it does have to be said that the marriage and family law is a lucky exception in law area and the jurisprudence of marriage and family is a lucky one in jurisprudence field. Even in the period of law uselessness and jurisprudence desolation, the marriage and family law and the jurisprudence of marriage and family were still treated well, which made it exist long in system and get lasting development in theory.

The marriage law in 1950 was the first law with the nature of the basic law issued after the establishment of the new China.[1]The "first" was not accidental, on

1 During the Women's Work Conference of Liberated Region held in Xibaipo in the autumn of 1948, LIU Shaoqi proposed that the Central Women Commission started to draft the first marriage law in New China. After the conference, the Central Women Commission immediately set up a group for drafting the marriage law. The Central Women Commission submitted the *Marriage Ordinance* modified for several times to the Central Committee of the Party in January of 1950. Subsequently, the Central Committee of the Party sent the draft of the *Marriage Ordinance* to variety of the democratic parties, the Central People's government, CPPCC National Committee, Law Committee, Committee of political sand law, Committee meeting of Political Affairs of Government Administrative Council and the relevant judicial organs and mass organizations for opinions. On April 13, 1950, the director of the Central Commission of Legislative affairs, WANG Ming, submitted *The Draft Of Marriage Law Of PRC* to the seventh session of the Central People's government, and gave a *Report on the Drafting Reason and Process of Marriage Law of PRC.* After that, Chairman MAO Zedong issued Presidential Order of the Central People's Government, announcing the Marriage Law should be in force since May 1, 1950. See: HUANG Chuanhui . *The World Marriage: the Chronicle of Three Marriage Laws of the Republic.* Wenhui Press, the first edition of 2004.

the one hand, it was a demand of the majority of people especially women, after political and economic emancipation, eager to get rid of the oppression of the feudalistic family system in marriage and family; on the other hand, it was also an experience summary on marriage and family system reform and legal construction during the period of the revolutionary bases. The law enjoyed a high international reputation, which was hailed as "declaration of reviving female human rights" of the new China by foreign scholars.[1]

In order to ensure the smooth implementation of China's marriage and family system reform, the CPC Central Committee and the State Council respectively issued the important instructions on the implementation of the marriage law on November 25, 1952 and February 1, 1953, confirming March of 1953 as the National Implementation Campaign Month of the marriage law. The campaign made the marriage law be spread to thousands of households, at that time, the independent marriage had increased significantly and democratic and harmonious families had emerged in a large amount, and the concepts of marriage freedom and gender equality had gradually become the mainstream of social values. In the first half of 1954, the number of application of marriage registration in compliance with the statutory conditions accounted for 95% of the total amount in the 11 largest cities in China[2]. By 1957, independent marriage had generally come true in most parts of China, which was a great change of Chinese marriage status in the seven years since the promulgation of the marriage law. A survey data by the National Women Federation showed that the proportion of the harmonious families in China had reached 85% to 95% at that time. The proportion of independent marriage had accounted for 90% to 100% in most areas of provinces of Heilongjiang, Liaoning, Shanxi, Hubei, Jiangxi, Zhejiang, and so on. According to the statistics by the Supreme People's court, the number of marital dispute cases accepted by nationwide

1 *Introduction to Female Science*. Chinese Women Press, 1986 version, p.158.

2 Quoted in: WU Changzhen, WAANG Deyi, YANG Dawen (editor). *Marriage And Family Issues in Contemporary* China. People's Publishing House, 1990 version, p.39.

courts decreased year by year between 1953 and 1956, in which the marital cases in 1956 decreased by more than half than those in 1953. The examination on 2,650,000 pairs of marriage registration by the Ministry of internal affairs found that 95% of it were in compliance with the marriage law provisions[1]. By the middle of 1960s, the marriage and family system in China had realized transformation smoothly from democracy to socialism, and the socialist marriage and family system had been established completely.

In the current jurisprudence system of China, the marriage and family jurisprudence (family law) is a part of the civil law. At the beginning of the new China, influenced by the Soviet civil legislation and civil law theory, the marriage law was excepted out of the civil law system. Before civil code was not published yet in our country when the *Marriage Law* was promulgated and implemented firstly (1950). Moreover, marriage and family jurisprudence developed gradually into an independent legal branch discipline by the implementation, propaganda, research and teaching of the *Marriage Law*, independent out of the civil discipline. The marriage law in 1950 played an important guiding role on the establishment of the marriage and family law system in the new China. At that time some textbooks on marriage law in some universities were basically compiled and published in accordance with the stylistic rules of the "marriage law"[2], rather than

1 "The harmonious families increase and the number of marriage dispute cases decrease significantly: Independent marriage has been realized in most parts of China". *People's Daily*, April 29, 1957.

2 For example, in the two books of *Basic Issues of Marriage Law* (a textbook for undergraduates in Law Department of People's university of China compiled by YANG Dawen, LIU Suping in 1958) and *Notes On The System Of Marriage And Family* (published by People's university of China Press in 1963), on the basis of reviewing the history of development and evolution of the system of marriage and family, it set forth legislative spirit, task, function and basic principle of the marriage law in 1950, and focused on the marriage system, family relationship and divorce system in the marriage law. These textbooks basically laid the system of Chinese marriage and family textbooks, which lasted until 1980s. Reference to: MA Yinan. *Chinese Marriage and Family Jurisprudence in the 20th Century*. Issued in Chinese and Foreign Jurisprudence, 1998, Issue 2.

directly to copy the theoretical system of Soviet marriage and family law works and textbooks[1].

3.2 Characters of marriage and family jurisprudence research in this period

The promulgation and implementation of the marriage law in 1950 played a huge role in promoting the study of the marriage and family law in the new China. WU Changzhen put forward, the contents of marriage and family law research in China in the 1950s mainly included two aspects: "First, to attack the feudalistic marriage and family system with the features of forceful arrangement, male superiority and female inferiority, ignoring interests of children; Second, to promote the new democratic marriage system with freedom of marriage, gender equality and protecting the legitimate rights and interests of women and children."[2] MA Yinan further pointed out that in this period the theoretical research by the marriage and family law scholars mainly served three major tasks: the first was to attack the feudalistic marriage and family system and its ethic discipline as value concept and theoretical system; the second was to expose the hypocrisy of the bourgeois marriage and family system and to resist the invasion of bourgeois marriage and family ideology; the third was to disseminate Marxist marriage and family theory and to provide a theoretical basis and guidance of public opinion for the implementation of the marriage law[3].

Through articles on the newspapers and magazines, textbooks and monographs

1 In the 1950s, a number of works of Soviet scholars were translated and published in China, such as, XU Fuji (editor & translator), *Essence of Soviet Family Law*, Shanghai Dadong Press, 1949 version; Swiltroff. Y.M. (editor), FANG Cheng (translator). *Soviet Marriage-Family Law*, Authors' Bookshop, 1954 version; Swiltroff. Y.M. (editor), LI Shikai (translator), *Legislation Principle of Soviet Marriage and Family*, People's Press, 1953 version.

2 WU Changzhen, *Marriage And Family Jurisprudence*, Issued in: ZHANG Youyu (editor), *Chinese Jurisprudence Research in the 40 Years*, Shanghai People's Press, 1989 version, p.403.

3 MA Yinan, *Chinese Marriage and Family Jurisprudence in the 20th Century*. Issued in *Chinese and Foreign Jurisprudence*, 1998, issue 2.

published in the 1950s, we can find out marriage and family jurisprudence research then closely surrounding the revolutionary task "abolishing the old and setting up the new" in the marriage and family field in the early establishment of the new China. So-called "abolishing the old" means to abolish the feudalistic marriage and family system; so-called "setting up the new" means to set up new democratic marriage and family system, namely socialist marriage and family system[1].Therefore, not only "the marriage law is an important weapon of revolutionary struggles in the field of marriage and family system"[2], but also the marriage and family jurisprudence research was inevitable to serve to achieve the revolutionary task.

The book *Chinese Revolution and Marriage & Family*, as one of master works in the field of marriage and family jurisprudence research at that time, highlighted the characteristics of the times from style to contents[3]. The author of the book MA Qi[4] thought, under the social background at that time, the purpose of researching the relation between Chinese revolution and marriage and family mainly reflected in three aspects: first, "setting up the view of marriage and family of Marxism Leninism, and practicing scientific analysis method"; second, "making clear the

1 WU Changzhen, *Marriage Law and I*, Law Press, 2001 version, p.7.

2 MA Qi, *Chinese Revolution and Marriage and Family*, Liaoning People's Press, 1959 version, p.87.

3 The book consists of six parts: Chapter 1, Research on purpose and method of marriage and family; Chapter 2, Origins and evolution of marriage and family; Chapter 3, Reform of Chinese revolution and system of marriage and family; Chapter 4, Revolutionary function of marriage law of PRC on the system of marriage and family; Chapter 5, Development direction of marriage and family of China; Chapter 6, Revolutionary task of the current marriage and family.

4 MA Qi (1904-1972), male, civil law experts and marriage jurist of the new China, held president of the senior court of Liaoning province, president of the senior court of Harbin province, president of the court of SongJiang province, president of civil division of North-East division of the supreme people's court, and so on. He was transferred to Law Department of North-East People's University (the former JiLin university), holding committee member of the university Party committee, the standing committee member of the university administrative committee, the first dean of the Law Department, adjunct director of the civil law research office. The materials comes from: http://xiaobao.jlu.edu.cn/newindex/read.php? id=738.

essence of the marriage and family forms and mastering the objective laws of development"; third, "sensing the legal spirit of policies, improving thinking and understanding, further to consolidate and develop the socialist marriage and family system"[1]. Based on this purpose, the method of researching the relation between Chinese revolution and marriage and family must be under the guide of Marxism materialist dialectics and the historical materialism, "to explore the essence of things through phenomenon, to analyze from the view of things continuously developing, to analyze from the point of class struggling and classes changing, also to analyze in the combination of each other from practice to theory and from theory to practice."[2] Starting from the discussion on the origin and evolution of human marriage and family system and after analyzing the characteristics of the old Chinese marriage and family system, he pointed out that the goal of the new Chinese marriage and family system reform was to eliminate the remnant of the feudal and bourgeois concept of marriage and family and to establish the socialist new democratic marriage and family. It had a detailed explanation on socialist marriage freedom, the basic aspects and features of the socialist democratic unity of family relations and the socialist divorce freedom, in which some understanding is still full of inspiration by reading today.

About socialist freedom of marriage, MA Qi thought three aspects of contents should be included: (1) the marriage freedom was concrete and essential freedom rather than abstract and formal freedom; (2) the marriage freedom was not the purpose but a means of realizing love and marriage; (3) the marriage freedom was not absolute, but relative, which would be subject to the restraint of law and discipline. He pointed out that the basic characteristics of the socialist family relationship were gender equality and the implementation of the monogamy. Overall gender equality in spouse relationship bodied that: Each party has freedom

1 MA Qi, *Chinese Revolution and Marriage and Family*, Liaoning People's Press, 1959 version, pp.4-5.

2 MA Qi, *Chinese Revolution and Marriage and Family*, Liaoning People's Press, 1959 version, p.6.

to career choice and participation in work and social activities; Each party has equal ownership and disposal to family property; Each party has their own rights to use their own names, and enjoys the rights to inherit property. The parenthood in an equal and democratic family shall be that "parents have the obligation of upbringing and education for their children; and children have the obligation to support and assist their parents; Both sides shall not abuse or abandon each other" (*Marriage Law*, Article 13). Adopted children and illegitimate children can enjoy the equal right to legitimate children. "The husband shall not abuse or discriminate the children who were born by his wife and her ex-husband and raised by his wife, or the wife shall not abuse or discriminate the children who were born by her husband and his ex-wife and raised by her husband" (*Marriage Law*, Article 16). The family relationship on the basis of equality and mutual assistance was different from the feudal old family relationships fundamentally in nature.

For the socialist divorce freedom, MA Qi firstly expounded the dialectical relationship between the divorce freedom and the marriage freedom. He pointed out that: "In order to achieve full marriage freedom, it must be at the time of implementation of the freedom of marriage, but also the implementation of the freedom of divorce; divorce freedom can complement the shortage of marriage freedom, and only if can the freedom of divorce carry out correctly, the freedom of marriage can play a greater role." Therefore, "If there is no freedom of divorce, there is no complete freedom of marriage, namely, if there is only freedom of marriage without freedom of divorce, it is equal to attaching the limit to the freedom of marriage and then it will lose the socialist basic meaning of the real freedom of marriage"[1]. He also thought that there were essential difference between socialist divorce freedom and bourgeois divorce freedom. Socialist divorce freedom had several basic characteristics: (1) divorce freedom with gender equality. No matter who was husband or wife, both sides had the right to

1 MA Qi, *Chinese Revolution and Marriage and Family*, Liaoning People's Publishing House, 1959 version, p.111.

request divorce in accordance with the law. (2) divorce freedom without prejudice to the interests of the collective. (3) divorce freedom with discipline. Anyone requesting divorce should be in accordance with the procedure prescribed by the law. (4) divorce freedom to consolidate the family relationship. Reckless divorce without careful consideration must be opposed, but random request for divorce without reason are also opposed, too.

MA Qi made interpretation on the implication of "if each of parties resolutely requests for divorce, and when it is invalid after mediation of District People's government and the judiciary, the divorce shall be granted", provided in Article 17 of the *Marriage Law*. He thought this was not as long as one party insisting on divorce, and regardless of the nature of contradiction between husband and wife, a divorce shall be granted unconditionally, "but depends on the demands of anti-feudal struggle and the basic principle of the reform and cultivation to socialist marriage and family, to deal with it in combination with specific situations." "Only its original marriage relationship is for too serious feudal factors indeed, or it is impossible to improve according to the socialist principles, if they continue, both interests of spouses and children would be seriously affected, and the development of social production would be hindered, can this kind of divorce be relieved."[1]

These perspectives of MA Qi indicated that the stability of the marriage and family relations in the early period of the new China was of great significance to the stability of the new regime. In order to safeguard the fruit of the revolution, the marriage and family jurisprudence research must serve the purpose. Therefore, for the theoretical problems in the marriage and family law, such as the freedom of marriage, the principle and limit of divorce as the academic points of view, it was inevitable to prominent political and classic quality. In spite of this, scholars generally believed that *Chinese Revolution and Marriage and Family* was a worthy representative of some scarce monographs of the marriage law in the

1 MA Qi, *Chinese Revolution and Marriage and Family*, Liaoning People's Press, 1959 version, p.117.

1950s. The book has laid a theoretical foundation for its later scholars' researches in the aspects of induction on the purpose and methods of researching marriage and family, on expounding systematically on the origin and evolution, on proofing on the connotation and relation of socialist marriage freedom and divorce freedom, and on description on the basic features of socialist family relationship.

3.3 Two theoretical hot spots of the marriage law research at that time

Although Chinese marriage and family jurisprudence owned a system model of developing research independently after the enactment of the *1950 Marriage Law*, we had to admit that the Soviet marriage and family jurisprudence had affected Chinese marriage and family jurisprudence at the early establishment of the new China, which mainly embodied on the understanding of many basic theoretical issues in the academic field, such as the issues of relationship between marriage and family law and civil law, the issues of the standard of divorce judgment, and so on.

3.3.1 Cognition to the relationship of marriage and family law and civil law

After the establishment of the new China, having inherited the legislation tradition in the period of revolution bases[1] and affected by the Soviet legislation, Chinese marriage and family legislation separated marriage and family law for adjusting personal and property relations between equality bodies in the human own production and reproduction field from civil law, as an independent law department. In works of Soviet scholars, we can see, marriage and family law was always a separate department in the Soviet legislation since the October revolution (1917), *Marriage, Family and Guardianship Code* promulgated in Soviet Union in 1918 and *Russian Civil Law* promulgated in 1922 didn't include the family

1 People's regime in the period of revolutionary bases focused using the law to reform the feudal marriage and family system. There were *Marriage Regulations of Republic of Chinese Soviet* in 1931 and *Marriage Law of Republic of Chinese Soviet* in 1934 in the period of the second revolutionary civil war. Regional Marriage Regulations were issued successively in various revolutionary bases in the periods of Anti-Japanese War and Liberation War, which laid a legal foundation for the promulgation of Marriage Law of the new China.

law, and special law for family relations stipulated in Article 3 of the latter's provisions, even the 1947 Soviet constitution made clear of the independence of family legislation (Article 14, Section 23). Soviet scholars believed that there were two reasons making the family law independent from the civil law: (1) the object of civil law was meant to the relation of property, but the object of family law was meant to the relation occurred in marriage, ancestry, adoption and children raising. (2) in the socialist society, family still retained some functions of economy, but it was not economic units of society. Therefore, processing the relationship of marriage and family needed some different norms from civil law. Of course, it was not said that all the norms of civil law were not applicable to family relationship. But the norms applicable to civil law had individuality in the family relations, mainly family property relations. And "only there were not expressly provisions for this issue in family-marriage legislation, and only application of civil law norms did not violate the basic spirit of family law, the norms could be applicable"[1].

The Soviet scholars' understanding of the relationship between marriage and family law and civil law had a direct impact on the establishment of Chinese scholars' views. Since in the early 30 years after the founding of new China the planned economy had been implemented, which made families lose economic function gradually, made people believe generally that Chinese family life had nothing to do with the economic life. In the meantime, in Chinese legislation guiding ideology and jurisprudence theory research Chinese scholars had emphasized one-sided on class nature of the marriage and family law, and had taken an attitude of negation and exclusion on the legislation in the countries of continental law system from form of technology to specific institution. They thought that taking marriage and family law as component of civil law was to make relation of marriage and family commercialized and contracting, and was the embodiment of the bourgeois will and interests, but taking marriage and

1 Swiltroff (editor), *Soviet Marriage-Family Law.*,Authors' Bookshop, 1954, p.31.

family law as an independent law department could embody advancement and revolutionary spirit of the socialist marriage and family law. So in a very long period of time, scholars in law circles generally believed that civil law was a law only to adjust commodity economy relationship, but marriage and family relation was not commodity relation, so it could not be classified into adjusting scope of the civil law, then marriage and family law, one of the three major components of the civil law, was separated from the category of civil law artificially[1].

In the 1950s-1960s, this understanding had a considerable representation, and the impact on China's civil legislative style for more than 30 years, which theoretical background was nothing but two: one was the one-sided emphasis on the class nature of marriage and family to exclude the legislation style in the countries of continental law system; the other one was the one-sided understanding to relation between marriage and family law and the civil law. The characteristic of marriage and family law as a special law of civil law had been magnified indefinitely, even it had become a major reason for its independence from civil law.

3.3.2 The dispute of "view of proper reason" and "view of affection breakdown" on the standard of divorce judgment

The 1950 Marriage Law was a system guarantee to relieve the feudal forced marriages, to achieve the freedom of marriage and to promote women liberation. Between 1953 and 1956, divorce cases accepted by courts all over China accounted for about 60% in civil cases in those years, ranking first in all kinds of civil cases[2]. At that time, some people had questioned to the divorce trial work of

1 It is a pity that editors have not found works on the relation between marriage and family law and civil law by Chinese scholars in the 1950s and 1960s in my writing process. Some relevant scholars and experts believed that at that time there were unified understanding in the academic circles, so no one wanted to argue the clearly basic theoretical issues. So in this book, I quoted the understanding on this issue in Soviet scholars' works temporarily as exemplification.

2 See: HAN Youtong, "Analysis and Suggestions On The Current Divorce Issues". *People's Daily*, April 13, 1957.

the people's court, thought that the court granting too much divorce fomented the rise of divorce rate; others thought haunting of bourgeois ideology was the main reason of divorce at that time, so such divorce should not be permitted.

On April 13, 1957, HAN Youtong[1]issued an article in *People's Daily*, in which she put forward her own view on the main reasons of divorce at that time, how to understand and deal with divorce issues and how to deal with divorce cases for the court. She argued that in the nationwide scale, when the main reason of divorce was still the feudal marriage relation and remnants of the feudal; and marriage was based on love, "when couples could not continue to live in common for spouse affection was completely ruptured, then such spouse relation was only existing in name, as a result, it was suffering for both sides, children and the whole family to keep this kind of nominal spouse relation reluctantly"; the court judging divorce should take it whether spouse affection had ruptured indeed as standard. "The court judging divorce depends on whether it is possible to reconcile spouse relation itself or not and whether spouse affection has broken completely, in essential, divorce or not depends on spouse relation itself, not on subjective desire of the court." "The court cannot simply judge divorce according to the feudal marriage or independent marriage, and it also can not judge it dis-permitted divorce for opposing impure ideology of one party involved or making mistakes on sexual liaison issues, which is like doctors doing surgery on patients with appendicitis, that doctors can not refuse to do surgery because the reason of causing appendicitis is that the patient eats too fast or too full." "On the contrary, no matter what the reason is, when the affection of two sides has completely been broken, and they can not continue to live together, the judgment of must-

1 HAN Youtong(1908-1985), female, after the establishment of the new China, held the posts of vice-president of North-China branch of the supreme people's court, vice president of civil division of the supreme people's court, president of the senior people's court in Ningxia Hui Autonomous Region, executive committee memeber of Chinese National Women Federation, master of the law group of the national committee of the CPPCC, vice director of institution of Law of Chinese Academy of Social Sciences, and so on.

not-divorce by the court will be a piece of useless waste paper." Therefore, a conclusion made by HAN Youtong: "By law, judgment of divorce or not is only used as a means of deciding existence or elimination of rights and obligations between spouse, but it shall not be used as a means of sanctioning wrong idea or behavior." Thus Han became a representative of "view of affection breakdown".[1]

HAN Youtong's views caused great repercussion in the academic and practical circles. "View of proper reason" was just in sharp contrast to this view. An article of "*On Understanding and Dealing with the Current Divorce Issue*" wrote by LIU Yunxiang was published on "*Jurisprudence*" in 1958. He argued that "the bourgeois marriage perspective and small bourgeois marriage perspective" was the main reason for divorce. He was opposed to satisfy divorce request on the basis of bourgeois ideology, and proposed that "if a party has destroyed the communist morality seriously, violated faithful obligation between spouse, or had other illegal or criminal behavior, making the marital relationship deteriorate, even causing the other party to ask for a divorce hereby, the people's court shall support and meet the requirements of the justice. If the guilty party puts forward a divorce, then the other party will have the right to decide the result"[2]. Thus LIU Yunxiang became a representative of "view of proper reason".

The magazine of *Chinese Women* opened up a column in 1958, unfolding a discussion on the two different views: "view of affection breakdown" and "view of proper reason". In an article signed in teaching and research office of civil law of the law department in Peking university published in the *Chinese Women* (Issue 4) aiming at different views on the issue of judging divorce standard between "view of affection" and "view of reason", they pointed out that, in a variety of divorce reasons, the feudal and the bourgeois ideologies would occur alternatively,

1 See HAN Youtong, "Analysis and Suggestions On The Current Divorce Issues", *People's Daily*, Apri 13, 1957.

2 LIU Yunxiang, *On Understanding and Disposal of the Current Divorce Issues Correctly*, quoted in: Civil Research Office of Politics and Law University of China compiled *Selected Articles on Marriage and Family Issues (the second volume)*, August of 1983, pp.434-435.

which were incompatible to the socialist marriage view, that such would cause the breakdown of marriage and family; "When the court are dealing with divorce cases, it should not only make clear of the divorce reason and the affection breakdown situation, 'based on facts', but also on the basis of the marriage policy of the Party and the state, 'taking the law as the criterion'." "It should not take affection and reason in opposition, and particularly it should not take apart factors of both sides and society relation.[1]" Meanwhile, an article signed in Editorial Department of "Jurisprudence" published on a magazine of "Jurisprudence" thought that it was one-sided, hypocritical and over-class view if we talked about spouse affection without politics, "the court shall depend on our country's marriage policy, making clear of what is against and what is to protect" when dealing with marriage disputes, rather than simply considering spouse personal affection, "first of all, the benefits of the other party, children and society shall be considered". The process of dealing with marital disputes by the court was a process of education, a process of improving the consciousness of the party with mistakes.[2]

This was the third view appeared in the debate process of "view of reason" and "view of affection", especially emphasizing on social function and political color of marriage, focusing on measuring social consequence with social interests and others' benefits, which was a comprehensive view in combination with the two previous views, herein it was called "view of combination of reason and affection" tentatively.

In the book of *Chinese Revolutionary and Marriage and Family* wrote by MA Qi, he also argued that view of "reason" or "affection" alone was "subjective

1 Civil Research Office of Law Department of Peking University: *Analysis and Comments on Divorce Issues*, quoted in: Civil Research Office of Politics and Law University of China compiled *Selected Articles on Marriage and Family Issues (the second volume)*, p.440.

2 "Jurisprudence" Editorial Office: *Treatment Suggestions on The Current Marriage Disputes*, quoted in: Civil Research Office of Politics and Law University of China compiled *Selected Articles on Marriage and Family Issues(the second volume)*, pp.444, 446-447.

and one-sided" in the process of dealing with issues of divorce. To grasp the limit of divorce policy correctly must depend on the nature and characteristics of different contradictions, and "connect three central links of dealing with divorce issues: namely, maintaining the socialist marriage and family system, protecting the interests of women and children and being conducive to the construction of socialist production, and solve specific issues with specific methods". "If having considered the nature of marital conflict, and having thought over the divorce requirement of the above three favorable aspects, it is an advanced requirement, for it is beneficial to persons and society, so it should be given support; on the contrary, ... that is a requirement lagging behind, which will damage the interests of the collective and hinder social progress, so it should be given persuasion and education, and the divorce request should be refuted"[1].

In the late 1950s, the theoretical controversy about standard of judging divorce in China's academic circle was the highlight of marriage and family jurisprudence research in this stage. It did not only push marriage and family jurisprudence research in the early establishment of the new China to a climax, but also let us appreciate a free-contention, theory-linking-with-reality, pragmatic and realistic academic atmosphere at that time. Facing the social reality is the life of jurisprudence research. Arising from judicial practice in trying divorce cases and ending in basic theoretical issues of marriage and family jurisprudence, this controversy also exposed the inadequacy of *The 1950 Marriage Law*. If *The 1950 Marriage Law* defined expressly the legal conditions to approve a divorce by the people's court like *the 1980 Marriage Law*,[2] this warm-atmosphere and view-

1 MA Qi, *Chinese Revolution and Marriage and Family*, Liaoning People's Press, 1959 version, pp.119-120.

2 No stipulating explicitly the principle foundation of the divorce approval by the people's court in Article 17 of Chinese "1950 marriage law" was the dispute source of legislative system between "view of proper reason" and "view of affection breakdown". It stipulated in Term 2 of Article 25 of the "1980 marriage law" that, "the people's court shall mediate on the trial of divorce; it shall approve to divorce if affection has broken down and the mediation is invalid."

distinctive academic controversy would not happen probably and a discussion on "affection view" and "reason view" was developed in academic theoretical circle again when the new marriage law was being formulated after the year of 1978. In the end, *The 1980 Marriage Law* took "couple affection having indeed broken" as the boundaries of the principle for the court to approve of divorce. This is the charm of jurisprudence research, for it does not only explain or note on the current national legislation, and make logic induction, deduction and reasoning on legal phenomenon, it also considers the actual needs and problems of social life, taking specific theories and ideas as a guide to lead the progressing direction of social consciousness and national legislation. It is necessary to mention that, the results of the academic controversy happened in the fifties of the 20th century was that "view of proper reason" took the superior position undeniably in the academic circle.

4. Chinese Economic Jurisprudence Under the Evolution and Reflection of Soviet Economic Law Theory

Before the reform and opening up to the world outside, the key words like socialist transformation, socialist revolution and construction, "the first five-year plan" in 1953, "Great Leap Forward" in 1958, three-year consecutive natural disasters since 1959, taking grain as the key link, taking steel as the key link, taking class struggle as the key link and the "Cultural Revolution" and so on, had become a vivid description on the economic and social history in this stage after the founding of the new China. In the first 30 years of jurisprudence of new China, the acceptance and inheritance from Soviet theory of jurisprudence in the law circle originated directly from the identification and copy of the ideology and the national system of the Soviet Union. A word said by the Communist Party of the Soviet Union then like this, "The October Revolution helped advanced people around the world, and it also helped the Chinese advanced people, who could use the proletarian universe outlook as tools to observe the fate of a country and reconsider their own problems. Follow the Russians' road—this is the conclusion"[1].

However, various kinds of theory and ideology of economic law schools with great influence at that time in Soviet Union had not been rooted in China. On the one hand, this was mainly due to China's jurisprudence locating in the political, economic and social environment then; on the other hand, this was mainly attributed to Chinese jurisprudence itself then being lack of rational critical spirit and introspection. Looking through China's jurisprudence textbooks or works, the mainstream view of Soviet jurisprudence were focused one after another, and class and tool value of law were repeatedly extruded and emphasized, but its social value was neglected or even denied seriously.[2] "The law in the Soviet Union was a powerful tool for the maintenance of the interests of the working people, the suppression of the exploitation of the classes, the organization of the socialist economy and the education of the working people."[3] Under the guidance of the jurisprudence ideology, the relationship between law and economy was also connected closely together with politics and policy, that is, the law was a means for serving politics, a specification and codification to the national policy. Specifically, it was the embodiment of the party's policies.[4] In this side, departments like penal code were like this, and some law on economy was also like this. Though some economic laws and regulations were also enacted, the policy legalization and law policy-oriented issues were still very prominent, so there had not been subjective and objective conditions to generate Chinese

1 *Address by Comrade MiKoyan, head of delegation of the Soviet Communist Party* (Speech on The Eighth National Congress of the Communist Party of China on September 17, 1956). The State and Law theoretical research office of People's University of China (editor). *Reference Material For State and Law Theory*, People's University Press, 1957 version.

2 More sadly, during the "Cultural Revolution", legal nihilism prevailed to disaster, so that the development of jurisprudence had to fall in stagnation and withering.

3 WANG Yongfei, *Reference Material for Jurisprudence Basic Theory*, volume 1, Peking University Press, 1982 version, p.535.

4 See: GAO Chengxiang, *On the Relationship Between Law and Policy*, issued in *Democracy and Legality*, 1979, issue 1.

economic law yet.

The issues of economic law was put forward in the legal circle of the Soviet Union when discussing how to treat different economic elements in 1920s, and accompanying with the fierce debate on the civil law and the economic law. Shortly after the 1922 *Russian Civil Code* was announced, some influential jurists in the Soviet Union looked the civil law as the synonym of the economic law, or included the civil law in the concept of economic law then.[1] From the 1920s to the 1960s, before and after, there were a total of five major schools in the development history of Soviet economic law, namely: (1) Method of two components. It was proposed by the famous jurist Stu Cheka. The economic law at that time had been distinguished from the civil law and excluded the civil law in essence, until 1938, the civil law had been excluded outside the syllabus and legal language all the time, which was not unrelated to increasing of the proportion of Soviet public components then.[2] (2) Prewar economic law school. It appeared in the middle of 1930s, whose representative was Genzbulga, Basu Kanis, and so on, and it believed that economic law did not only adjust the relationship between socialist organizations, but it also adjusted the relationship between citizens.[3] (3) the postwar economic law school, also known as the modern economic law school. Created by the famous economic jurists Laptsev and MamouTov firstly, it put forward that economic law was used to adjust various relations formed in guiding and organizing economic activities between the socialist organization and its subordinate departments, which such relationship was called economic

1 CHEN Hanzhang, *The Fifty-year Debate between Soviet Economic Legal School and Soviet Civil Legal School and its Experience and Lessons* (serials), *Chinese Jurisprudence*,1985, Issue 2.

2 See: Isaev, *Economic Law in Soviet Jurisprudence System in the 1920s*, CHEN Sui (translator), CHEN Hanzhang (proofreader), issued on *Jurisprudence Translations*, 1985, Issue 5, originally issued on *Soviet Countries and Law of Soviet Union*,1982, Issue 2.

3 See: XIAO Jiangping, *Research on the history of Chinese Economic Jurisprudence*, People's Court Press, 2002 version, p.69.

relations, occurring in the process of socialist reproduction.[1] (4) comprehensive subject economic law. Taking Yoffe and Schall Gerald as its representatives, it thought that economic law belonged to the comprehensive legal subject, without a unified adjustment object and method, which was not an independent law department (later Yoffe abandoned view of the comprehensive legal subject).[2] (5) the economic administrative law. It was proposed by the well-known experts in civil law, BoLaToosi etc. in 1963, and put forward that economic law was just the economic administrative law, and economic law was just administrative law for adjusting the relationship of economic management, and administrative and civil relations could not be confused in the "economic law".[3]After decades of debate and evolution, these schools had gradually been divided into two major groups: the civil-administrative law school and the modern economic law school. Many of their opposite views in many fields of economic jurisprudence could be reflected in definition of "economic law" and its basic property: civil-administrative law school held the view of general economic law basically, and thought that economic law did not have the attribute of department law, and citizen was one of bodies of economic law; while the modern economic law school held the view of narrow economic law, which excluded financial law, land law, labor law outside, and thought that economic law was only to adjust part of economic relations, namely a law of economic management sections and enterprises, engaging in economic activities and leading economic activities occurring relationship between each other, which was a unified and independent legal department, and citizens could not become its main body. Furthermore, there were also many opposite views in the adjustment way, the goal and the principle, the economic

1 B.B. Laptev (author), YING Shichang (translator), SU Ning (proofreader), *Economic Law: Object, Way, Purpose and Principle*, *Contemporary Foreign Philosophy Social Science Digest*, 1985, Issue 1.

2 See: XIAO Jiangping, *Research on the history of Chinese Economic Jurisprudence*, People's Court Press, 2002 version, p.69.

3 See: C.H. BoLaToosi, *On Pathway of Economic Legislation Systematization*, *Selected Essays on Soviet Economic Law*, Law Press, 1982 version, pp.95-108.

contract, the economic law discipline education and so on.[1]

The theory and system about the Soviet economic law theory above, has reflected the background of economic policy, economic system and economic system in different economic development stages in Soviet Union, in which there was also isomorphism with Chinese economic institution then. The planned economic system of the new China at the early founding stage was a product of the state power to intervene the economy by force. The establishment of the socialist public ownership and the operation of the planned economy system were carried out under the protection of the state power. Power was glued together with the planned economy closely and firmly, and the state was endowed with the power of unified leadership, unified planning and management to the financial and economic work, and then further the state was made sure a dominant position in the national economy development. Such as in public finance and fiscal law field, after negating the old China's theory of "public finance" completely, China began to use Marxism methodology to re-understand the essential issues of the finance, through the introduction and questioning "theory of monetary wealth" and "theory of monetary relations" of the Soviet Union, and gradually formed "theory of state distribution" taking the mainstream status in the planned economy period, which the government revenue was mainly constituted by the business tax and profit enterprises paid, such that the state participated freely into the distribution of part of social products or national income with a body identity for realizing its functions. No wonder that ZHANG Wenxian valued when commenting on market economy and the legal construction: "The planned economy is essentially a power (administration) economy." In the planned economy system, politics and economy were integrated into a whole, in which economy was the dependency of politics, and producers did not have independent ownership and management rights, and lateral subject relationship did not occur between producers actually, and what

1 See: XIAO Jiangping, *Research on the History of Chinese Economic Law*, People's Court Press, 2002, p.69.

was left was only longitudinal affiliation between superiors and government. Government mainly allocated resources depending on administrative power, administrative orders, job arrangement with grades, red head files or laws and regulations as an extension of the administrative power, to command production; and it also depended mainly on administrative organs to arbitration, mediation or decision with administrative means, without need to get the aid of judicial procedures, when there were economic controversies or economic disputes. This made it minimal of the function of the law based on justice and equality in the planned economy.[1]

However, it was very strange that when China inherited and accepted the Soviet jurisprudence theory in a large scale, but the Soviet economic law theory at the same period had failed to enter the legal profession and legal practice in China in a system form. The historical reason was worthy of finding. In a period after the founding of new China, law subjecting to politics was emphasized, legal theory and practice could not avoid beginning to fall into this or that misunderstanding area. Such as Chinese politics between 1957 and 1976 was full of class struggles and a series of political movements, though Chairman MAO once said that politics was the concentrated expression of economics, he did not still take economy as the working focus of the party. In view of this, although there had been translation versions and introductions to the former Soviet economic law in China academic circles[2], the Soviet economic theory had not widely spread into Chinese jurisprudence practice and influenced it in 1950s. In view of the reason, the first was that the Soviet jurisprudence had influenced China a lot in the early 1950s, but what was introduced and accepted was mainly the mainstream jurisprudence theory with Vyshinsky as the representative, which was reflected

1 See: ZHANG Wenxian, *The third Comment on Market Economy and Legal Construction*, *Chinese Jurisprudence*, 1993, Issue 3.

2 For example, in the *National News Weekly* in 1927, Volume 4, Issue 43, there issued *Soviet-Russian Economic Law* translated by HAI Shi, and in No.229 of *Chinese and Foreign Economy Weekly*, there published *Soviet-Russian Economic Law Regulation*.

in the constitution, criminal law, criminal procedure law, marriage and family law, land law and labor law, more in department law research, and because the theory of economic law was often treated as "poison" in the Soviet Union, it was impossible to be introduced and spread into China naturally. The second was that in the late 1950s, when the Soviet Union began to re-understand the economic theory formed in 1930s, China and the Soviet Union began to split. So, there was no opportunity to introduce and spread Soviet economic law theory in China appearing in the 1950s. After entering the 1960s, while the Soviet economic law theory influenced the Eastern European countries in different levels, it began to affect China indirectly.[1]One of its manifestations was that the Civil Law Department of People's University of China drafted "*The Economic Law of the People's Republic of China (Draft)*" in March of 1963. Although the draft had only 70 articles, its structure was clear, and the system was complete, so it could be regarded as a complete code draft. According to the provisions of Article 1[2] and Article 3[3] of the draft, all of the economic activities of all organizations and citizens were taken in the adjustment range of the economic law[4], from which we can see the influence of the economic law theory of the Soviet Union.

It should be said that, as jurisprudence of other departments, the research on issues of economy and law of the new China in the legal profession was still mainly concentrated in the first ten years after the founding of the new

1 Reference to: LI Xiuqing, *On the Influence of Soviet Economic Law Theory on China*, Politics and Law, 2002, Issue 3.

2 This article prescribes: This law is a principle of various organizations and citizens economic activities made on the basis of socialist construction general line of the Communist Party of China and constitution of PRC.

3 The term prescribes: who having the right to participate in various relations adjusted in this law, enjoying the rights in accordance with the law and burdening the obligations is the following organization or person: (1) Various organizations with independent accounting or budget, and burdening independent property responsibility. The law prescribes that organizations established through registration process can participate in various relations adjusted in the law. (2) Citizens of the people's Republic of China.

4 Reference to: LI Xiuqing, *On the Influence of Soviet Economic Law Theory on China*, *Politics and Law*, 2002, Issue 3.

China. In the next 20 years, legal researchers had been marching forward in misunderstanding area, namely, taking "the great leap forward", the critique of bourgeois jurisprudence view, anti-imperialist and anti-revisionism and other political movements as the main task of jurisprudence research starting from the point of view of the class struggle, the error of "left" deviation had developed increasingly, which had missed unnecessarily the good opportunity created for jurisprudence health development after the completion of "the first five-year plan" successfully, resulting in that jurisprudence career did not only develop in a normal logic, but shrink continually, until the annihilation in a series of political movements. Naive class feelings, political chanted slogans, rigid doctrines of preaching, romantic revolutionary ideal, a high degree of political critical enthusiasm and furious moral indignation had replaced the contents of the law itself.[1]Therefore, the study on the theory and evolution of economy and law can only be locked in the first ten years after the founding of new China, and in the ten years, and this issue is the focus of the study of many civil law scholars. For the economic law, the concept of "economic law" was introduced into China early in the 1920s[2], the introduction contents of which had been involved the reason of formation of economic law in Germany, different views of the concept of economic law of German scholars and the nature and scope of economic law, but these results did not cause attention in the law circle of China. After the founding of new China, due to various subjective and objective reasons, it was lack of introduction and analysis of Soviet economic law theory in the law circle of China, and the real prosperity of Chinese economic law happened after the end of the 1970s. While China began to reform and open up with the orientation of reforming the system of planned economy, however, the Soviet economic law reflecting the Soviet planned economy characteristics made significant inroads

1 See: CHEN Jingliang, *Several Issues In Jurisprudence Research Of the New China - Based On A Survey Between 1957 and 1966*, *Jurisprudence Research*, 1999, Issue 3.

2 *The New Era Product—"Economic Law"* was serially issued in the column of "Foreign Legal News" in the Issue 26 and Issue 27 of "*Law Review*" in December of 1923.

into Chinese economic jurisprudence field like living from the death, which was a strange place of the history.

5. Research on the Establishment of the Socialist Judicial System

Like other legal disciplines, the research on new Chinese socialist judicial system, on the one hand, was originated without foundation under the political background of abolishing the old law system; on the other hand, based on the prevailing social environment, ideology environment and international political situations, it was influenced far-reaching on the establishment research for the construction of China's socialist judicial system by the Soviet legal theory. The two objective situations have determined the characteristics of research related to the judicial system in this period.[1]

5.1 Learning and referring to the Soviet judicial system theory and research methods

As the preliminary establishment time of the socialist judicial system research in the New China, the research work of scholars in this period was mainly carried out by translating, learning, introducing and referring to the Soviet judicial system and the jurisprudence theory of Russia civil lawsuit and criminal lawsuit. Such as, the Ministry of justice of the Central People's government published a book named "Soviet judicial practice" in November of 1951, in which the relevant literature on the judicial system of the Soviet Union and its specific actions were included, namely the activity principle, organizational structure and authority of

1 This part is mainly referred to: ZHANG Youyu (editor), WANG Shuwen (associate editor), *Chinese Jurisprudence in the Forty Years*, Shanghai People Press, 1989 version; CHEN Guangzhong (editor), *Criminal Litigation Jurisprudence in the Fifty Years*, Police officer Education Press, 1999 version; CHEN Ruihua, *Chinese Criminal Litigation Jurisprudence in the 20th Century*, *Chinese and Foreign Jurisprudence*, 1997, Issue 6; CHANG Yi, TIAN Pingan, HUANG Xuan, LI Zujun, *Review on the Fifty-year of Civil Litigation Jurisprudence in New China and Prospect*, *Modern Jurisprudence*, 1999, Issue 6; XU Hui, *The Past, Present and Future of Civil Litigation in Mainland Area*, Published in "Law Institute of 'Chinese Institute' in Taiwan, China", *Law Development in the Four Regions Across the Straight* (Volume 2), New XueLin Press in Taiwan, China, 2007 version; HE Qinhua, *Reflection on the transplantation of Soviet judicial system in China*, *Chinese and Foreign Jurisprudence*, 2002, Issue 2.

the Soviet judicial organs, Soviet lawyer constitution, Soviet-Russian National Notary Association, the organization and activities of the Soviet Supreme Court, the organization and activities of the Soviet comrades trial conference, the inspection work of the Soviet judicial organs, research on trial practice in the Soviet judicial organs, organization of the Soviet legal education, organization of the consolidation and codification of code in the Soviet judiciary organs. The book was used as a reference for the study of judicial cadres. The East-China Branch of the Supreme People's court and the East-China Branch of the supreme prosecution department jointly compiled and published "The speech record of Soviet expert: Comrade Runev on the court, procuratorial work in East China region" in August of 1954, as a textbook for internal learning and reference, including a total of twelve pieces of speech, in turn as "organization and internal division of labor of Soviet prosecuratorial organs", "general supervision scope and method", "adjudication supervision", "relationship of the division of labor between the procuratorial agency and the court, the police, supervision, and other departments alike", "special procuratorial agency and the special court", "the problems about rural and urban procuratorial work", "on the Soviet criminal and civil cases lawsuit proceedings", "three issues on the lawyer system, the notary system, the comrades trial conference", "keys to other specific issues", and so on.

In the aspects of referring to and learning the judicial system and theory of the Soviet Union, Chinese scholars translated and published a large number of Soviet judicial system monographs and textbooks wrote by the Soviet scholars in 1950s.At the same time, in order to improve Chinese judicial system, the civil and criminal lawsuit code of the Soviet Union and other Eastern European "people's democracy" countries were translated and published in China. Of the more important textbooks and Monographs in the Soviet judicial system translated and published, some had more significant influence like: ZHANG Junti (translator) "*Soviet-Russian Criminal Procedural Law*" (Xinhua Bookstore, 1949 Edition); WU Daye (translator) and CHEN Zhongcheng (proofreader) "*A History of Lawyer System of the Soviet Union*" (Public Law Press, 1950 Edition); XU Buheng (translator) "*Outline of the Soviet Procedural Law*" (Public Law Press, 1951 Edition); Cheri Geoff(author),Criminal research office of People's University of China(translator) "*Criminal Procedural Law*" (Volume 1 and 2, People's University of China Press, 1953 Edition); the cadre training group of Committee on politics and law of the Central People's Government Administration Council (compiler) "*Legal Profession Course Syllabus for the Soviet Union Law School*" (issued in 1954); Ann Jan Vyshinsky (author), WANG Zhixiang (translator) "*the Soviet Legal Litigation Evidence Theory*" (People's Press, 1954 edition); Abramoff (author), Judicial research office of People's University of China (translator), "*Soviet Civil Procedure*" (Volume 1 and 2, Law Press, 1956 edition); "*Curriculum Syllabus for 'the Soviet Court and the Procuratorate Organs'*" (for the higher school of law, People's University of China press, 1955 edition); Klingman, C Vallee Va (compilers), CHEN Yiyun (translator), "*Soviet Civil Procedure Outline*" (for the higher law school, Renmin University of China press, 1956 edition); Lebe Kinski, Tarja Vo (compiler), XUE Bingzhong (translator), "*Curriculum Outline of 'the Soviet Chief Prosecutor's Supervision'*" (Renmin University of China Press, 1956 edition); Kleman(author), WANG Zhixiang, WANG Zengrui (translator) "*Soviet Civil Action*" (Law Press, 1957 edition); Schaffman (compiler), XUE Bingzhong (translator) "*The Soviet Criminal Litigation Internship Textbook*" (Renmin University of China Press, 1957 edition); Gu Woolwich (author), KANG Baotian, SHEN Qichang (translator) "*Litigious Rights*" (Renmin University of China Press, 1958 version), and so on. At the same time, a number of Chinese scholars and students were sent to the Soviet Union for studying and learning the Soviet legal system and legal theory; some famous jurists in the Soviet Union were dispatched to China, teaching the Soviet Union's legal theory and judicial system.

The introduction of the Soviet jurisprudence theory had had a great impact on the construction of Chinese legal system of jurisprudence theory and research methods. Such as in the theoretical study of the civil judicial system, the distinction between public law and private law was denied, and the nature of private law in civil legal relationship was negated, so it made the court have the right to intervene disposition of the private right fully of the involved party in civil proceedings. According to the Soviet jurisprudence theory, in the socialist countries, there was only public right and no private right. Even if it was the civil rights of individual citizens, still without more private color, so that all social legal relationships were public relationships and had no private law relationships, namely so-called “we do not recognize any ‘private’ things, in our opinion, everything in the economic field belongs to the scope of public law, but not anything private...So the intervention on ‘private law relationship’ by the state must be expanded, and the power of the state to abolish ‘private person’ contracts must be expanded too; Our revolutionary legal consciousness rather than the Roman law should be applied to ‘civil legal relationship’.”[1]In accordance with the theory of the state and the law of the Soviet Union, the court was just a tool for the state, an agency serving for the interests of the state. Now that there was no distinction between public law and private law, the state had the power to intervene on activities in the traditional civil relations field. Therefore, both the courts and the procuratorial organs would have the power on behalf of the state to intervene in the disposal of private rights of the involved parties.[2]

Meanwhile, in the study of the criminal justice system, the research methods of party spirit and the class nature of the Criminal Procedure Law was emphasized. In accordance with the point of views widely accepted by the Soviet scholars, “there is not the supra science or the supra party spirit and it hasn’t ever appeared”, “Soviet criminal litigation is a science with the party spirit”, which regarded “Lenin’s and Stalin’s theories about the dictatorship of the proletariat, the doctrine of the functions and the tasks of the Soviet states, and the Bolshevik party policy” as the starting point. At the same time, Soviet criminal litigation science and all of the science of law of the Soviet Union, were “a part of a new system of thoughts, namely a part of the superstructure on the basis of socialism”,

1 *Lenin Manuscript*, Volume 4, People Press, 1963 version, pp.222-223.
2 Reference to: Kleman, *Soviet Civil Litigation*, Law Press, 1957 version.

which regarded "the tasks proposed by the Soviet Communist Party (Bolshevik) for the Soviet people and countries as the starting point" when solving all the problems of theory, but also according to the whole experience of the Soviet state construction in the implementation of the trial. The above nature of Soviet criminal litigation determined that it could not apply that kind of research position and method of the supra-class "objectivism" and "cosmopolitanism", instead, it should take materialist dialectics as "the only right" research methods.[1]Based on this, when explaining the nature of "the criminal litigation science of PRC", "*The Criminal Litigation Syllabus of PRC*" enacted in 1956 clearly pointed out that "Marxist dialectics is the scientific method in researching the criminal litigation science", emphasizing the "party spirit of the criminal litigation of PRC", and requested to understand clearly the "difference of the essence between the criminal litigation of PRC and that of the bourgeois states". What's more, the last two chapters of the syllabus held an attitude of negation and critics on "the criminal litigation of the bourgeois states" and "the criminal litigation of the reactionary Kuomintang government", but a positive attitude on "Soviet criminal litigation" and "the criminal litigation of the people's democratic countries". Adhering to the viewpoint of the party spirit and class nature of research of criminal litigation must inevitably result in a widely application of the research method of class analysis. In the 1950s and 1960s, big discussions on issues of criminal evidence having class nature or not were launched in Chinese criminal litigation law circle, in which there were quite many scholars pointed out explicitly that the criminal evidence was the tool to realize the class interests and will for the ruling class, therefore, it had strong class nature.[2]At that time, the materialist dialectics had been used to research the issues whether the criminal

1 Cheri Geoff, *Soviet Criminal Litigation*, Law Press, 1956 version, pp.40-44.

2 Reference to: XU Yichu, *Introduction to the Research of Criminal Litigation Jurisprudence*, Tianjin education press, 1989 version; CUI Min, editor, *Introduction to Research of Criminal Evidence Theory*, Chinese people's public security university press, 1989 version.

evidence had subjectivity, and whether it was "a unification of the subjective and the objective contradictions" in the criminal litigation law circle. The reasons of the phenomenons of academic history could be attributed to the influence of the legitimacy of the research method to Chinese criminal litigation jurisprudence.[1]

5.2 The formation and experience accumulation of the judicial idea under the idea of criticizing the old and developing the new

At the beginning of new China, a judicial reform movement with the main contents of opposing the "old law" view, the old judicial style and the reform of the judicial organs at all levels were carried out widely in the legal profession and the judiciary circle. The legal system and the jurisprudence theory of Kuomintang were negated and criticized thoroughly according to Marxist view, standpoint and methods in the jurisprudence circle and the judicial circle, and the theory of state and law were set up as the fundamental guiding ideology of the jurisprudence research. At the same time, some judicial work experience in the former CPC liberated area were also widely spread and concluded. "Relying on the masses, and following the mass road" was promoted as a good tradition of the people's judicial work.[2] In this stage, the judicial system formed in the first half of the twentieth Century was abandoned from the theoretical system to the research results and research methods.

In the field of criminal justice, while the law circle and the judicial practical departments carried out the criticism to the old law, they also carried out the criticism to the old system of litigation in particular, drawing clearly the principle boundary between the new and the old judiciary and its litigation system in theory and constantly enhancing the cultivation of the theory of the state and the law, and having removed the obstacles in ideology for the construction of the new criminal litigation jurisprudence. However, under the historical condition at that time, there

1 CHEN Ruihua, *Chinese Criminal Litigation Jurisprudence in the 20th Century, Chinese and Foreign Jurisprudence,* 1997, Issue 6.

2 CHEN Ruihua, *Chinese Criminal Litigation Jurisprudence in the 20th Century, Chinese and Foreign Jurisprudence,* 1997, Issue 6.

existed the shortcomings of negating simply all of the old law ideology and the old litigation system in the critics.[1]

In the field of civil justice, for the inheritance and development of MA Xiwu trial mode carried out by the Shaan-Gan-Ning government of border region during the period of revolutionary bases,[2] mediation was regarded as a civil judicial principle in the theoretical research of civil judicial system. As the characteristic of the new justice under the new system and the new China then, it was not only to stress solving civil disputes through mediation, but also required to the implementation of the mass justice, because MA Xiwu trial mode was regarded as the real people's justice. The sixteen-character principle of "relying on the masses, investigation, mediation, solving on the spot" in the work of civil trial replaced the civil procedure law in the modern sense, when the principle was surrounded mainly to develop the research of the civil justice system."To do the civil trial work as masses of work, and to do it as the ideological and political work"[3]was advocated at that time. Therefore, at the time of implementation of the mass line into the judicial process, judicial formalism and tedious procedure rules were abandoned and abolished, in this case, the civil justice was no longer a specialized

1 ZHANG Youyu, WANG Shuwen, *Chinese Jurisprudence in the Forty Years*, Shanghai People Press, 1989 version, pp.252-253.

2 MA Xiwu trial mode was the best summary to trial experience in various border area and revolutionary bases, which was characterized by emphasizing highly on mediation. MA Xiwu (1899-1962), the creator of "MA Xiwu trial mode", was born in Zhidan county, Yan'an city. He attended revolution in 1930 and joined in the Party in 1935, having held the posts of Minister of Ministry of Food in ShanGan worker and peasants democratic government, Minister and President of Ministry of national economy.He held commissioner of Qinghuan Prefecture, that of Longdong Prefecture, president of Longdong divisional court of the supreme court in Shaan-Gan-Ning border area. "MA Xiwu trial mode" created by him was supported by the masses and promoted in liberation area. He took the post of president of the supreme court in Shaan-Gan-Ning border area in 1946. After the founding of PRC, he took the posts of president of North-west divisional court of the supreme people's court, adjunct vice president of the politics and law committee of North-west military and administrative commission and vice president of the supreme people's court.

3 *A report at the Second National Conference on Civil Judicial Work by Ceng Hanzhou, Vice President of the Supreme People's Court* (December 22, 1978).

activity, and the role division between judges and the audience was not obvious, even not necessary to be divided, so the civil litigation had been ideological and political work with going deep among the masses, investigation, unlimited in forms, persuasion and education, and the resolution to civil disputes had become activities of preaching and persuasion, uniting the masses of the ideology. Because of this mass justice having great flexibility and randomness, the compliance and construction of civil litigation procedure had been greatly restricted.

5.3 The exploration of the establishment of the theoretical system of the Chinese socialist judicial system

Through study and reference to the Soviet jurisprudence theory and judicial system, the theoretical system of the Chinese socialist judicial system has gradually been established. Between July of 1955 and the second half of 1958, the courses of criminal litigation and civil litigation were produced into classes in variety of departments of politics and law, and textbooks were also compiled, such as the people's University of China published "*Chinese Civil Litigation Notes*" and "*Soviet Criminal Procedure Teaching Syllabus*" (Chinese version) as textbooks, and many other colleges and universities copied and reproduced these textbooks.

At this stage, some articles researching Chinese judicial system also came out one after another, and Chinese scholars also carried out a thematic discussion on some issues in the system of the civil litigation, criminal litigation and judicial system, as a result, about a hundred of papers were issued. The problems explored in these papers were relatively concentrated on mainly the judicial organization and its principle, the court's independent trial, defense system, status of the This paper examines the problem of relatively concentrated, mainly in the judicial organization and the principle of independent trial, defense system, proceedings status of the parties concerned, evidence and so on. However, in the aspects of introduction and reference to Soviet judicial system and litigation jurisprudence theory, its purpose of theoretical research and demonstration to investigate was not a theoretical investigation in need of Chinese litigation practice, but to illustrate and confirm the rationality of the Soviet litigation jurisprudence theory, and criticizing "the tedious nature and anti-people nature" of legislation, theory and practice of civil and criminal judicial system in the old China.

Since then, with the influence of the 1957 "anti-rightist" movement and legal nihilism, there were so many academic forbidden zones that scholars could not, and did not manage to be engaged in theoretical research. Jurisprudence theoretical research was in stagnation basically. Because people could not only research legal issues freely, but also the podium notes by teachers must go through reviews one after another in the legal nihilism prevailing period. In the "1958 great leap forward" period, a guideline was put forward that "Teaching shall serve the proletarian politics, education shall be combined with productive labor", due to the influence of the "left" thought, resulting in that some extreme actions were taken in jurisprudence educational area, such as regarding jurisprudence talents in the cultivation goals as "ordinary workers", carrying out the system of "half work, half study", and emphasizing study in "working", and greatly reducing the professional courses. Since the mid of 1960s, due to the revocation of departments of politics and law, the theoretical research about jurisprudence was not only stagnated thoroughly, but also some scholars and experts were persecuted, so that the only several jurisprudence periodicals like "*Research on Politics and Law*", "*Translation Compilation of Politics*", "*Jurisprudence*" were forced to stop publication shortly after their establishment.[1] The very incomplete theoretical research system of the socialist judicial system having been initially established was completely destroyed by the environment of policy and society then. However, this kind of theoretical research method and guiding ideology of learning and reference to Soviet judicial system developed up in 1950s had not been abandoned due to the interrupt of its history, but it got revivification and development and its influence has been lasting until today.[2]

1 CHANG Yi, TIAN Pingan, HUANG Xuan, LI Zujun, *Review on the Fifty-year of Civil Litigation Jurisprudence in New China and Prospect*, *Modern Jurisprudence*, 1999, Issue 6.

2 CHEN Ruihua, *Chinese Criminal Litigation Jurisprudence in the 20th Century*, *Chinese and Foreign Jurisprudence,* 1997, Issue 6.

This book is the result of a co-publication agreement between China Social Sciences Press (China) and Paths International Ltd (UK)

This book is published with the financial support of Chinese Fund for the Humanities and Social Sciences (本书获中国国家社科基金中华学术外译项目资助)

Research on the Laws of Contemporary China Volume 1: 1949-1978
Editor-in-chief Chen Su
Translated By He Jingjing and Shang Cong
ISBN: 978-1-84464-484-1
Ebook ISBN: 978-1-84464-485-8

Paths International Ltd
PO Box 4083
Reading
United Kingdom
RG8 8ZN
www.pathsinternational.com

Published in the United Kingdom

CPSIA information can be obtained
at www.ICGtesting.com
Printed in the USA
LVHW101422070519
616597LV00005B/36/P

9 781844 644841